```
B          McCall, Edith
SHREVE
           Mississippi
             steamboatman


    $11.95                    3028
```

DATE			
OCT 26 '90			

MORNING CREEK ELEMENTARY SCHOOL
10925 MORNING CREEK DRIVE SO.
SAN DIEGO, CA 92128

© THE BAKER & TAYLOR CO.

Mississippi
Steamboatman

Henry Miller Shreve

Mississippi Steamboatman

THE STORY OF HENRY MILLER SHREVE

Edith McCall

ILLUSTRATED WITH PHOTOGRAPHS AND ENGRAVINGS

Walker and Company
New York

Walker's American History Series for Young People
Frances Nankin, Series Editor

Frontispiece: Portrait of Henry Miller Shreve, approximately sixty-four years old, his snag boat visible in the window.

Copyright © 1986 by Edith McCall

All rights reserved. No part of this book may be reproduced or transmitted in any form or by any means, electric or mechanical, including photocopying, recording, or by any information storage and retrieval system, without permission in writing from the Publisher.

First published in the United States of America in 1986 by the Walker Publishing Company, Inc.

Published simultaneously in Canada by John Wiley & Sons Canada, Limited, Rexdale, Ontario.

Library of Congress Cataloging in Publication Data

McCall, Edith S.
   Mississippi steamboatman.

   (Walker's American history series for young people)
   Includes index.
   Summary: A biography of the riverboatman who, among other achievements, designed and built the first steamboat able to navigate the Mississippi River.
   1. Shreve, Henry Miller, 1785–1851—Juvenile literature. 2. Naval biography—United States—Juvenile literature. 3. Inland navigation—United States—History—19th century—Juvenile literature. 4. Steam-navigation—United States—History—19th century—Juvenile literature. [1. Shreve, Henry Miller, 1785–1851. 2. Boatmen. 3. Steamboats—History] I. Title. II. Series.
VM140.S57M36   1985   623.8′2436′0924 [B] [92]   85-13795
ISBN 0-8027-6597-1

Book Design by Teresa M. Carboni

Printed in the United States of America

10 9 8 7 6 5 4 3 2 1

ACKNOWLEDGMENTS

Little has been written in recent times about Henry Miller Shreve. There are no collections of his letters and personal papers, except for the official correspondence and reports from his service as United States Superintendent of Western River Improvements. The only other known writings of Captain Shreve are his 1838 patent application and *A Memorial,* a small book published in 1847. These contain details of his invention of the snag boat, helpful in the preparation of this book.

Other treasure-troves were files of old newspapers, such as *Niles' Weekly Register* (1814–20) and *Fifty Years on the Mississippi,* by E. W. Gould (1889), as well as a brief biography of Shreve in *U.S. Magazine and Democratic Review* (1848). I am also indebted to the authors of numerous secondary source books of steamboat history.

For help in obtaining illustrations, I appreciate the assistance of Captain Fred Way, Jr., steamboat captain and historian, and of Lloyd Hawthorne, artist, student of history, and fellow believer in the need to give recognition to Shreve for his work. Grateful acknowledgment also goes to the National Portrait Gallery, Washington, D. C.; the *Shreveport Times* and the Norton Art Gallery of Shreveport, Louisiana; the Ohio River Museum, Marietta, Ohio; the Mariners' Museum, Newport News, Virginia; and the Mercantile Library, St. Louis, Missouri.

LIST OF ILLUSTRATIONS

Frontispiece, portrait of Henry Miller Shreve
Map, the inland rivers in early steamboat days, circa 1840
The *Vesuvius*, built by Robert Fulton in 1814
Henry Miller Shreve's *Enterprise*
Map of the Falls of the Ohio, Louisville, Kentucky
Henry Miller Shreve's *Ohio*
The Mississippi River in early steamboat days
Shreve's "floating palace," the *George Washington*
Shreve's snag boat, the *Capt. H.M. Shreve*
"Captain Henry M. Shreve Clearing the Great Raft from Red River, 1833–38"
St. Louis, Missouri, riverfront scene circa 1840
Statue of H.M. Shreve, Shreveport, Louisiana

Contents

Introduction	1
Chapter One	7
Chapter Two	16
Chapter Three	28
Chapter Four	37
Chapter Five	48
Chapter Six	58
Chapter Seven	71
Chapter Eight	81
Chapter Nine	90
Author's Note	99
Henry Miller Shreve, 1785–1851: A Chronology	104
Living History	109
Photo Credits	111
Index	113

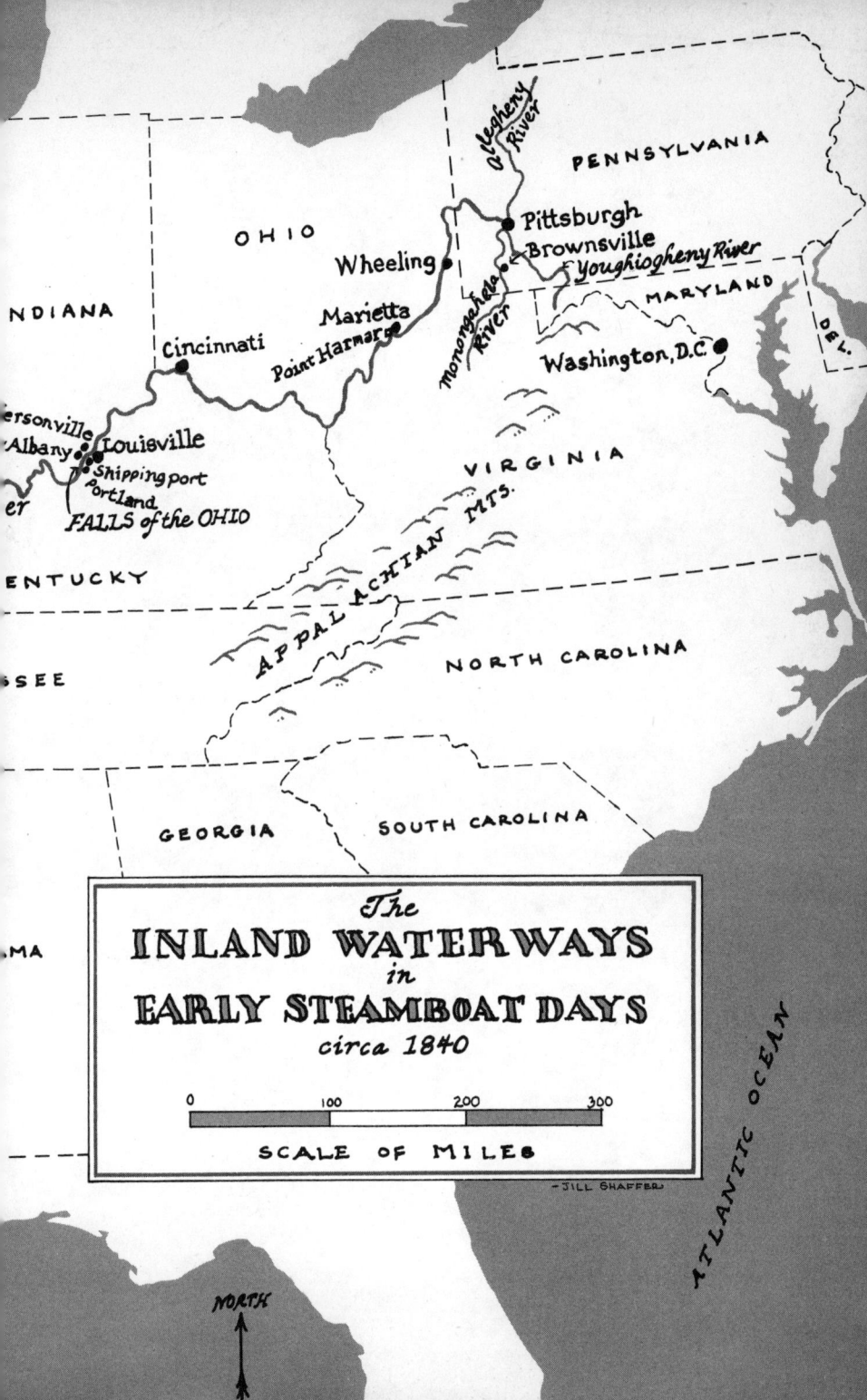

Introduction

THIS is the story of an American riverboatman who had an inventive mind and plenty of persistence. Without wealth or political power, he did more than any other person to improve transportation on America's inland rivers. His name was Henry Miller Shreve.

Henry Shreve built the first successful Mississippi River steamboats. Other steamboats, built by the eastern businessman Robert Fulton, could go down the Mississippi River but their engines were not powerful enough to go upriver against the difficult currents. Henry Shreve designed a steamboat that could do the job. With little money, and often working against strong opposition, he did not give up, even after a damaging explosion on his steamboat's maiden voyage. His invention brought practical and profitable steamboat transportation to inland America.

From the start, Shreve had to fight for the right to use his steamboats. His boats were blocked from free trade in Louisiana waters by a law that gave all trade to Robert Fulton's company. Shreve risked everything he had when he took his fight to Louisiana's courts. He won free trade on the rivers for all Americans.

When Shreve reached middle age, he faced another challenge. The rivers, choked with dangerous driftwood that cost lives and damaged boats, had to be cleared. Putting his inventive mind to work on the problem, Shreve designed the steampowered snag boat. Again his invention succeeded, and his work helped open the way for progress and growth in a newly settled America.

When Henry Shreve was born in New Jersey on October 21, 1785, George Washington had not yet become president. Most Americans lived along the Atlantic coast, between the ocean and the Appalachian Mountains. Henry's father, Colonel Israel Shreve, had fought with General Washington in the Revolutionary War. When the war ended, his New Jersey farm was in ruins. Like many other people, Colonel Shreve decided to move to the West, which at that time meant west of the Appalachians.

Henry was not quite three years old when his father formed a wagon train and moved his family and some friends to southwestern Pennsylvania. The place Colonel Shreve chose was in Fayette County, southeast of Pittsburgh. He bought sixteen hundred acres of land from George Washington who, before the war, had built a log house and gristmill there.

To Henry, the farm and mill were less important than the fact that his home was between two rivers. Rivers held a fascination for him, and they continued to do so all his life. The Shreve farmlands reached eastward to the Youghiogheny River—called the Yough for short. About five miles to the west was the Monongahela River, often called the Mon.

The Yough flows into the Mon about twenty miles above Pittsburgh. At Pittsburgh, the Mon meets the Allegheny River, and together they form the Ohio River. The Ohio flows westward to meet the mighty Mississippi. Throughout his life these rivers—and the adventurous life they represented—beckoned Henry.

There were boat builders working near the rivers, and Henry spent as much time as he could watching them construct the boxy crafts called flatboats. Sometimes he would ride a horse to Brownsville, the largest town near his home, located on the Mon. He would go to the riverfront hoping to find keelboats, which he liked better than flatboats. Flatboats were used to take people and goods downstream, but they were too clumsy to bring back upriver against the currents. Keelboats, in contrast, were two-way vessels. Built on a keel—the long slender timber that ran the full length of the boat—a keelboat's shape was designed for less resistance to the river currents. These boats were pointed at both ends and somewhat rounded on the bottom. Keelboats were the best riverboats made in those days. They were used to take frontier products down the rivers to cities where they were needed and to bring back products to the farmers and people of the upriver cities.

When Henry Shreve's father died in December, 1799, Henry knew what he wanted to do. He got a job on a flatboat to learn the skills of a boatman. As soon as he had enough experience, he planned to work on a keelboat and save his money to buy one. In 1806, Shreve became a boatowner and was given the title of captain. He was twenty-one years old.

At that time, the United States was mostly a vast, unexplored territory. After the Revolutionary War, the Mississippi River was the western boundary, but in 1803 hundreds of thousands of acres were added with the Louisiana Purchase. All the land drained by the Mississippi River system, including the Missouri River and its branches, became part of the United States. In all that territory, there were no towns except a few near the west bank of the Mississippi. St. Louis was one of these—a trading village just below the mouth of the Missouri River.

Captain Shreve went to St. Louis with his first keelboat in 1807. No one from Pittsburgh had traded there before, and Shreve pioneered a good business. Three years later, he went farther up the Mississippi to buy lead from the Illinois Indians. They mined the heavy metal in what is now northwestern Illinois. Captain Shreve made enough money to buy a larger keelboat in 1811. He also got married and bought a house in Brownsville.

During this period, pioneers in ever growing numbers were moving west to the land between the Appalachians and the Mississippi River. Some pushed farther west into Missouri. As land was cleared and planted, the settlers were able to produce more than they needed. They had products to sell. These western products were wanted in the cities along the east coast. In addition, settlers wanted things from the East that they could neither grow nor make. They were ready to trade, but they had one problem. There was no simple way to transport their goods to the East and bring back the goods they wanted.

There were no roads west of Pennsylvania except for very short wagon trails and, of course, there were no railroads. But there were plenty of rivers. The Mississippi, the Missouri, and the Ohio rivers combined with their many tributaries to form a network across inland America.

At New Orleans, Louisiana, near the mouth of the Mississippi, goods could be transferred to and from ocean-going ships. The answer to the transportation problem was to move the goods by boat. That was how the East and West could trade.

Henry Shreve's large keelboat, and others like it, offered the best in river transportation. It took six weeks, however, to travel south and west from Pittsburgh, Pennsylvania, to the port city of New Orleans, and more than four months to make the return voyage. The loaded boat had to be pushed with poles or dragged by a tow rope a distance of about two thousand miles. The only power in use on the inland rivers was the muscle power of brawny men.

There was hope, however, that steamboats would be built for use on the Ohio and Mississippi rivers. In 1807, Robert Fulton's *Clermont* was put into service on the Hudson River in New York. There were rumors that Fulton and his partner and financial backer, Chancellor Robert R. Livingston, would soon be building steamboats for the inland rivers. For young

Captain Shreve, who was forced to make the long, slow voyage up the Mississippi, the day couldn't come too soon!

The first Fulton boat built for the inland rivers came down the Mississippi in 1811. It could not, however, make the upriver voyage and was turned back at Natchez, Mississippi, by strong, swirling currents. No other boat could make the attempt because other steamboat builders were not allowed to do business in Louisiana, where the important seaport city of New Orleans was located. Chancellor Livingston had agreed to bring steamboat power to Louisiana solely on the condition that the Fulton-Livingston boats be the only steam-powered boats allowed to use Louisiana's rivers. His condition was made into law.

This meant that when another company built a steamboat, it would not be allowed to bring goods to New Orleans or reload with goods to take back upriver. A company might be licensed to trade in Louisiana, but the license fee, set by the Fulton-Livingston company, was too high. After it was paid, there could be no profit for the boat owner. The law allowing this monopoly seemed unfair to Shreve and other riverboatmen who hoped to change over to steam power. They felt that the rivers belonged to all people, not to a chosen few.

As if these were not problems enough, there was also great danger that the city of New Orleans would soon be closed entirely to American shipping. The United States went to war with England in 1812. Americans were tired of the British seizing their sailors and forcing them to serve in the British navy. They were tired of them giving American Indians guns and gunpowder, encouraging frontier attacks on white Americans.

As the War of 1812 progressed, the United States lost many battles. It appeared that England would win. By autumn of 1814, English soldiers and marines approached New Orleans, threatening to capture the city. If they succeeded, the supply route to inland America would be cut off.

As our story begins, young Captain Shreve is deeply involved in these situations. He has three strong desires. One is that the war will end with victory for the United States, keeping the city of New Orleans an American port. Another is to be forever through with the drudgery of keelboat operation and be the master of a steamboat. The third is to find a way to break the Fulton-Livingston monopoly on steamboat trade.

In the autumn of 1814, Captain Shreve has become one of the owners of a steamboat being built at Brownsville. He has decided he will fight the Fulton-Livingston monopoly and use his new steamboat in Louisiana. On his last keelboat voyage to New Orleans, he realized there was great danger of losing the port city to Britain. His plan is to use the new steamboat to help save New Orleans, and begin his own steamboat trade in that city.

One

QUIETLY, trying not to awaken the rest of his family, Captain Henry Shreve closed the front door of his home behind him. It was the day he'd been looking forward to for years, yet he had an uneasy feeling. Would he ever go through that doorway again?

The chill of a gray, wintry dawn struck him and he pulled his dark blue boatman's coat closer. Setting his captain's cap firmly on his head, he slung his pack over his shoulder and started down Front Street. Then he turned to look at his house. Mary, his wife, waved to him from a window in the shadowy half darkness. He waved back and walked briskly down the street, heading toward the Monongahela River.

He had often left home this same way in the nearly four years of his marriage, and for eleven years before that. Ever since he was fourteen, when he became a riverboatman, he had been heading out on long voyages, but this day, November 30, 1814, was different.

Last night, when Mary seemed worried, he had pretended there was no great danger in what he planned to do. Just the same, he had to admit even he was uneasy about what lay ahead.

Never mind, he told himself. His step grew firmer. Lean and strong, he squared his shoulders as he started down the hill. After all, this was the day he'd waited and planned for. Today he was making the long voyage to New Orleans by steamboat. He refused to allow the dangers of wartime to ruin his triumph.

Halfway down the hill his boat, the *Enterprise*, came into view. It was docked in the Mon, easily visible with its big smokestack and two tall masts. Henry looked for his crew members who should have come aboard the night before. None were in sight, but he was greeted by an old friend, Daniel French, as he drew near.

French had designed and built the *Enterprise* and was one of Captain Shreve's partners in the boat's ownership. The two men went down the steep slope to the river. The water lapped quietly against the seventy-five-foot hull of the gray boat. They walked up the gangplank. French would not be going along, for his work was here in Brownsville. He was building another steamboat, somewhat smaller than the *Enterprise*. Its hull was nearly complete. Sometimes French envied the men who had the excitement of traveling on the boats, but he knew that his work as designer and builder was just as important. On this morning, he went aboard for one last quick check of the machinery.

Shreve dropped his duffel bag on the deck, took off his cap, and ran his fingers through his thick brown hair. As he turned to face his friend, French saw an unfamiliar look of worry in Henry's eyes. He asked no questions, for he knew what was on the captain's mind.

When Shreve had left New Orleans in July and started up the Mississippi, everyone knew the city would be attacked sooner or later. British ships had blockaded all the seaports, stopping American ships from entering or leaving the harbors. It was common knowledge that British soldiers were positioned along the Gulf of Mexico, but the people of New Orleans didn't know when or how the attack on their city would come. Though they were told that General Andrew

Jackson was trying to fight his way through to defend the city, no one knew just when he and his soldiers would arrive.

"We'll have to fight with everything we've got!" one of the militia members had said to Captain Shreve in July. The militia were the volunteer soldiers who drilled to be ready to help the regular army when the attack finally came.

"Trouble is, we haven't got enough," another said. "Even when General Jackson gets here—if he makes it in time—we'll still be short on men. Even worse, we don't have enough guns and lead and gunpowder! And with the British blockade, we can't get any from the East. The only way anything can be brought to us is down the river on boats like yours, Captain Shreve."

It was then that Shreve had decided that, instead of spending the winter back in Pennsylvania as he usually did, he would load a boat with munitions at Pittsburgh and then return to New Orleans.

"I've got a steamboat all ready for me up in Pennsylvania," he told the militiamen. "I can use it to get back in a hurry with a full load of munitions."

Soon after Shreve returned his keelboat to Brownsville, the *Enterprise* pulled into its home port for checking over. Thrilled, Captain Shreve had taken her down the Mon on practice runs, loving the feel of the mechanical power.

And now the time had come to start. He was to take the helm as master for the long downriver voyage, into the scene of whatever battle there was waiting for him.

"Good luck, Henry." It was all that Dan French could say as he turned and went back down the gangplank.

"Every man hit the deck!" Shreve called out, cutting into the morning quiet. Soon all was hustle and bustle as preparations for departure were made.

Down in the hold, chunks of firewood lay stacked, ready to keep the fires burning for several days. The engineer was ordering crewmen to build a hot fire in the firebox for the boiler. When the water in the boiler was hot enough, steam would escape into a cylinder and be held there until the pressure gauge showed almost forty pounds. Then there would be enough steam power to operate the machinery that turned the paddle wheel at the stern, or back of the boat.

Daniel French watched from the water's edge as the gangplank was pulled in. Captain Shreve took his place in the pilot house. Blowing the curved brass horn he had used for years on his keelboat, Shreve signaled that the steamboat was about to embark.

"Oo-ooo-oo!" It was a smooth yet sad sound. Shreve blew two more blasts.

The ropes were untied and crewmen pushed the steamboat out into the water, clear of the dock. Steam hissed from the safety valve and then stopped as more valves were opened to let the steam power the machinery. The paddle wheel, with much groaning, clanking, and splashing, began to turn.

As the steamboat started down the Mon, Dan French was no longer alone on the dock. The sounds had attracted other Brownsville people, and they cheered the *Enterprise* on its way. Captain Shreve waved from the window of the pilot house before he turned his full attention to guiding the boat.

The Mon, like all the rivers in those days, had not had its channel cleared of snags—the logs and even whole trees that had been torn loose from the riverbanks at floodtime. Some lay only partly open to view and would appear above the water briefly and then disappear. These were called "sawyers" because of their up-and-down sawing motion. Running into any of these could rip open a wooden boat hull, and Captain Shreve had no intention of letting that happen on his first steamboat voyage.

Keeping his eyes on the river ahead, Shreve spoke to his mate, who stood beside him at the helm. "On to Pittsburgh, John. We'll be there in three hours, if we move along like this. Sure beats poling down in a keelboat."

"She'll ride even better when we have a full load of cargo," John replied. He, along with other crewmen, had sailed the *Enterprise* during the summer months. The entire crew, except for two young boys, were experienced riverboatmen. Several stood on guard with poles to push aside any large pieces of driftwood they came upon as the boat moved along. The bo'sun, the man who stood near the prow or front of the boat, was responsible for signaling to Captain Shreve when he saw dangerous looking snags ahead. He made it possible for the captain to steer the boat clear, and the success of the voyage depended on his sharp eyes. The captain was constantly on the alert for any hand-signal his bo'sun might make.

Whenever they passed a village along the way, people waved their hats from the riverbank. News had spread of the *Enterprise*'s mission to help save New Orleans. The steamboat ran beautifully, and in what seemed but an hour or two they were at the outskirts of Pittsburgh.

"Look, John!" Shreve called out. "There's another boat in the cradle at the Fulton-Livingston boatyards." He pointed to

The *Vesuvius*, built in 1814. This was the second of Robert Fulton's steamboats to travel down the Ohio and Mississippi rivers.

his right, where a nearly finished steamboat stood in the water. It was almost twice as large as the *Enterprise*, and the name *Aetna* was on its newly painted hull.

"She's just like the *Vesuvius*," the captain said scornfully as they steamed past the boatyard. *Vesuvius* was the name of the second steamboat the Fulton-Livingston company sent down the Ohio. "And she probably won't do any better in the Mississippi River. The Fulton boats are all built like ships."

"I noticed that, Captain. Must be those New York boat builders think that's the way to build a steamboat."

"They're built for deeper water than we have out here!" Shreve exclaimed. "That's one of the reasons the Fulton boats have so much trouble. They have a hard time keeping clear of the sandbars." Shreve stopped talking for the engineer had lowered the steam pressure and the paddle wheel was turning more slowly. The *Enterprise* was approaching the landing at Market Street.

Shreve's mate went down to the main deck as the boat eased into position at the dock. Crewmen took up poles, guiding her close.

"All right, boys. Snug her up." The two crewboys tossed the rope ends to young boys waiting eagerly on the landing. Soon the ropes were tight and the *Enterprise*, with one last gasp of escaping steam, stood neatly at the Pittsburgh landing.

Captain Shreve prepared to leave the boat briefly to arrange for the delivery of munitions at the army depot, a short distance away. As he walked down the gangplank, a man approached him.

"Young man," the stranger said. "You are a brave fellow."

"Why do you say that?" Shreve asked.

"Well, Captain, I'd be afraid to ride on one of those steam-powered contraptions. That boiler could blow up and you'd never know what happened."

"I'm not worried about that, sir. We have several safety features to keep the steam pressure from getting too high." Henry made a move to leave, but the man took hold of his jacket sleeve.

"And the gunpowder you're taking on board? Anything could set it off. You'd be blown to pieces!"

Shreve looked hard at the man holding his arm. "That's a risk I have to take, sir. General Jackson needs munitions if he's to save New Orleans. And now, sir, I've got to go. Thank you for your concern."

Shreve tried to pull away, but the man held him, preventing him from leaving. "And if that isn't enough," the man added slowly, "you are going to New Orleans knowing that the Fulton-Livingston people are likely to take your boat. Perhaps you should reconsider."

Shreve stared for a moment, then pulled his arm free. "Believe me, they'll not take the *Enterprise!*" Shreve told the stranger. He was getting angry now. "I'm a fighter, too, you know—and besides, I've got a good lawyer working for me. No, sir, I'm not afraid, but thank you anyway. You'll see me— and the *Enterprise*—back here as soon as New Orleans is safe."

Shreve fumed as he hurried up Market Street. For a second he wondered if the stranger hadn't been a Fulton-Livingston man himself. But he dismissed the thought. He had work to do. He headed across town to the United States Army supply depot near the Allegheny River. Having left an order there several weeks ago, he needed to make sure the munitions were ready. He had ordered a full boatload of guns, gunpowder, cannon balls, bars of lead, and even some rifles if he could get them. Upon learning that the supplies were ready, he wasted no time in getting back to the *Enterprise*.

Pittsburgh is built on a triangle of land where the Allegheny River meets the Monongahela to form the Ohio. Sandbars are common and river currents are difficult. It took careful navigation for Captain Shreve to get the boat turned upstream into the Allegheny, but before long she was docked again alongside the army depot, and the loading began. Captain Shreve made sure that the kegs of gunpowder were packed carefully, and as far from the steam engine as possible.

"We'll be on our way early tomorrow," he told his crew. "Get a good night's rest."

* * *

And so, on December 1, the *Enterprise* began the long voyage to New Orleans. Seven hundred miles from Pittsburgh, the steamboat approached Louisville, Kentucky, and the most dangerous part of the Ohio River. Known as the Falls of the Ohio, this was a two mile stretch where the water flowed over ledge rock and boulders. The Falls were actually more like rapids. The water, as it went over this rocky riverbed, was quite shallow, and at times when the river was low, large boats could not go through this part of the Ohio. When Fulton's first steamboat, the *New Orleans*, had headed downriver, it had been forced to wait many weeks until the rains made the river deeper. Captain Shreve was grateful that his steamboat could go through without delay.

Before going over the Falls, every boat had to stop in Louisville to take on a pilot—someone who knew the safest way to go through the narrow channels. Shreve paid the pilot's fee, and the *Enterprise* was guided safely through. They stopped at Shippingport, a small settlement at the end of the rough water, to let off the pilot and were on their way again.

A few miles down the river, they passed a keelboat trying to come upriver. The boatmen were struggling along the shore, pulling the boat with a long tow rope over their shoulders. Shreve felt anew the joy of handling his steamboat. Only a few weeks ago, his own crew had been forced to work that hard, dragging his keelboat upriver. Perhaps before long more steamboats could bring an end to such hard labor.

They went on their way, carefully avoiding the many snags. Shreve knew the rivers well from his earlier voyages, and they made good progress. They reached the mouth of the Ohio and entered the Mississippi sooner than Shreve could have believed possible.

Just after they started down the Mississippi, they saw a convoy of three keelboats pulled over at a village. The crews seemed to be loafing in the midde of the day. Shreve had been told at Pittsburgh that these boats were also taking munitions to New Orleans. It bothered him that they seemed in no hurry. He blew a blast on his horn as the steamboat swept past them.

Farther along, a short distance above Natchez, Mississippi, Shreve saw the sandbar where the second Fulton inland river steamboat, the *Vesuvius*, had been stuck in July. The steamboat was not there, obviously freed by the rising waters. As they approached Natchez, the captain pointed out the sunken hull of the *New Orleans*, which had carried freight and passengers in the lower Mississippi River for two and a half years. It had been wrecked there, its hull pierced by a stump. The *Vesuvius*, if again afloat, would be the only other steamboat at New Orleans.

The *Enterprise*, her engines working beautifully with the current to help move her along, arrived at New Orleans on December 14. The voyage from Pittsburgh had been made in a record two weeks.

"Now we really get to work," Shreve said, "and let's hope we're in time!"

Two

As soon as the boat had docked, Captain Shreve called out to the crowd who had come to the levee to see the *Enterprise*. "Did General Jackson get here yet?"

"Yes! He's here!" came an answering shout, and several people added, "Thank God!"

"Got those munitions for us?" The question was from one of the militiamen Captain Shreve had talked with before his trip to Pennsylvania.

"That I have," Henry said. Then he noticed the *Vesuvius*, with no signs of life about her, a short distance down the waterfront. "What's the *Vesuvius* doing down there? Is she in trouble again? Looks as if she's listing a bit."

"She got back a couple of weeks ago—about the same time the general arrived—but she's hung up on a sandbar!" the militiaman answered.

"Hm-m-mph," was the captain's response. "That's 'cause she's built like an ocean ship instead of a riverboat."

But there was no time to be concerned with the troubles of the *Vesuvius*, for a group of aides sent by General Jackson came to take care of Shreve's very welcome cargo.

"The general wants to see you right away," an aide told

Shreve. He directed the captain to a three-story building on Rue Royale, where General Jackson's headquarters were.

Leaving John in charge of the unloading, Shreve climbed the gangplank to the top of the levee. This was a long earthen wall about fifty feet wide, built to prevent rising river waters from flooding New Orleans. Shreve had to push his way through a crowd, for the levee top was used as an open air market and people were selling everything from fresh vegetables and fish to tinware.

He made his way to the steps that led down to an open square, called the Place d'Armes. A militia unit was drilling there. Shreve walked past them and over to Rue Royale. When he arrived at Jackson's headquarters, a young lieutenant told him to be seated.

"Tell the general that Captain Henry M. Shreve has arrived, please."

"Yes, sir. But he's resting. He's been ill, you know. I don't want to bother him." He looked over toward a closed door.

After about ten minutes the door suddenly burst open. General Jackson did not look toward Shreve as he stormed over to the lieutenant's desk. Shreve studied the lean, weathered man whose thick shock of reddish hair was already streaked with white. He judged the general to be about fifteen years older than himself—somewhere in his forties.

Sharply worded questions, well mixed with swearing, were aimed at the young officer as the general tried to learn what had happened to some keelboats, due weeks ago with military supplies.

"The British are closing in on us from all directions. How in tarnation am I to defend this city without men or munitions to hold them off?" The general pounded on the lieutenant's desk.

Shreve started to rise from his chair and Jackson saw him. "Who's this?" he asked.

Shreve answered for himself. "Captain Henry Miller Shreve, of the steamboat *Enterprise*, newly arrived in port with a cargo of military supplies, General Jackson."

Jackson turned to the lieutenant. "Why didn't you tell me he was here?"

Then he stepped toward Shreve and the two men shook hands. Shreve was surprised at the brilliance of Jackson's blue eyes as each man took measure of the other.

"I hope you can control your steamboat better than those on that useless *Vesuvius*, Captain Shreve. I told my men to keep watch for your boat's arrival and to get her unloaded immediately."

"They're doing that right now, sir. The *Enterprise* is smaller than the *Vesuvius*, but she's running and at your service. And I aim to keep her that way."

Jackson grunted. "And did you chance to see those keelboats?"

"Yes, General. I passed them about a week ago, just below the mouth of the Ohio."

"Fine. As soon as your cargo is unloaded, get back up the river and see that the supplies on those keelboats are moved down here quickly. Can't wait for them to poke along."

"Yes, sir. One more thing, General. I understand martial law is in effect here. Is that true?"

Martial law means that all people are to assist the military and obey the officers, instead of city and state law.

"Yes, Captain. You, your crew, and your steamboat are in my service until we win this blasted war."

"Does that mean that no one can take court action against me because of state laws?"

Jackson looked inquiringly at Shreve. "You been breaking some laws, young man? Well, no matter. Martial law is in effect, and my orders top all city or state laws."

"Thank you, General. I'll have the *Enterprise* back up the river as soon as possible." Shreve smiled as he turned to leave. Now he didn't have to worry about the *Enterprise* being seized by the Fulton-Livingston men—at least not until Jackson's work was done.

Back at the steamboat, he found the unloading almost completed. "Fire up again, men," he said. "We've got to go back upriver and find those keelboats we passed near the Ohio."

Though Shreve said nothing to his crew, he was worried that the *Enterprise* might have difficulty against the upstream currents. Though his boat was equipped with a higher pressure engine than those on the Fulton boats, this would be its first true test. Time would tell. . . .

He sounded three blasts on his horn, and the big paddle wheel began its reverse turn. Slowly—carefully—the steamboat backed into deeper water and turned about.

"So far, so good," Shreve muttered as he handled the big wheel. "Full speed ahead, mates!"

The *Enterprise* did have some difficulty when it met the swirling currents at Natchez four days later. But Shreve's knowledge of the currents, and the fact that the river level was high, helped him navigate them. Twelve miles above Natchez, they found the keelboats.

"We'll tow them downriver," Shreve told John. "Prepare for a turn-about. We'll stop about a quarter mile below the keelboats."

The turn was made, and the keelboats slowly came into position along the shore behind the steamboat.

"We're taking you in tow—General Jackson's orders," Shreve told the keelboat captains as the cables were secured. "Get ready for a fast ride, boys. We'll be in deep water most of the way, so you'll be safe, but keep your poles ready just in case!"

Six days after they left New Orleans, they were back. They had traveled day and night to cover the six hundred and twenty-five miles.

"Now then," General Jackson told Shreve, "I'm going to keep you and your steamboat busy—you can count on that!" The general was pleased with Shreve's work, and he gave his next order. Shreve was to take supplies to troops stationed along the rivers wherever the water was deep enough for the steamboat. He was to begin with a trip down the Mississippi to Fort St. Philip. This fort was the most important of the outposts because any ship coming upriver from the Gulf of Mexico could be seen from it. Located on the east bank of the Mississippi River, it was halfway between New Orleans and the river's mouth, about fifty miles from the city.

Then, on December 23, there was great alarm among the people of New Orleans. British troops coming from the East had slipped through Jackson's guards. They had taken over a plantation about ten miles downriver from New Orleans, on the same side of the Mississippi. The British officers made the plantation house their headquarters, with their troops encamped on the grounds. It seemed obvious they were preparing for an attack.

Many men were worried about the safety of their families, now that a battle was sure to come. A group of them went to see Captain Shreve after he returned from one of his missions with the *Enterprise*.

An elderly gentleman, seeming to speak for the group, spoke to Shreve in a worried voice. "Captain," he said, "we have women and children whose safety concerns us. Would it be possible for you to take them upriver about fifty miles, to a plantation where they will be safe until this dreadful time is over? Our horses and carriages are all in the military service."

Shreve took off his peaked captain's cap and ran his fingers through his hair. He knew how these men felt—he would feel the same way if his wife and children were here.

"Folks, I'd take them on board in a minute, but the *Enterprise* and I are both under martial law. You will have to ask General Jackson. If he gives his permission, I'll do it gladly the first chance I get."

"Then we'll talk to the general today. Thank you, Captain."

When Shreve returned to the New Orleans waterfront late the next afternoon, the little committee was waiting for him. The general had given his permission.

Shreve checked in at Jackson's headquarters. "Any other assignment for me, General?" he asked.

Jackson was busy charting something on a map. Scarcely looking up, he said, "Nothing right now, Captain."

Henry Miller Shreve's *Enterprise* was the first steamboat to make the voyage from Pittsburgh, Pennsylvania, to New Orleans, Louisiana, and return. The voyage took place in 1814–1815.

Shreve told him of his plan to take the women and children to safety. "Since you have no need for me now," he said, "I'll tell them to get ready, and we'll head upriver first thing in the morning."

"Yes, yes," Jackson said, still looking at his map. "Go right ahead."

The committee was waiting at the *Enterprise*. "Have people and baggage at the landing at daybreak tomorrow. We'll take all that the *Enterprise* can carry."

In the morning, the people were there. They carried their clothing and other personal needs, as well as bundles of precious family belongings that they did not want to risk losing in an attack on the city. There were children and tiny babies with their mothers and nurses. There were elderly people and a few who were sick, but well enough to travel.

They were nearly all on board, the steam pressure building, when the young lieutenant from Jackson's headquarters came running.

"Captain Shreve! You can't do this now! The general wants you to report to him immediately. He has another assignment for you and your steamboat."

Shreve looked back at the women and children crowded helplessly on the deck of the *Enterprise*. He turned to the lieutenant.

"You go back and tell the general I'll be in to see him as soon as I get back."

"But Captain Shreve—you know how angry he'll be!"

"Let him fume. He told me I could take these people up the river, and he knows it. Now go and tell him."

The lieutenant turned away with a stricken look on his face. Shreve went back to getting the baggage moved into the cargo space and seeing that all passengers' names were listed. He was about to tell his crew to pull in the gangplank and cast off when a company of soldiers came marching up behind the uncomfortable-looking lieutenant.

"Seize him," the lieutenant ordered weakly.

Shreve came down the gangplank. "Now just a min—" He stopped when he found himself seized by the arms.

"About face! Forward march!" the lieutenant called out. "General's orders," he added in an aside to Shreve.

Two soldiers started to drag the captain. "All right, all right," Shreve said. "Let go of me. I'll go along—I've got a little something to say to the general myself!"

At Jackson's headquarters, the general turned to Shreve, red with anger.

"By thunder, Shreve, do you dare disobey my orders?" he shouted.

Shreve's eyes met the general's. "Yes, I do dare!" he shouted back. "I'm doing what you gave me permission to do, and by thunder, I'll do it. Those poor people are depending on me!"

The general stared at Shreve blankly. "What people?" he asked.

"The people you told me just last night I could take upriver, that's what people!"

Slowly, a look of understanding came across Jackson's face and he turned away. As he walked into his office, he said, "Report here immediately upon your return, Shreve."

But as Shreve saluted and started to leave, the general couldn't help adding, "And make it fast."

When he returned the next morning, Shreve caught a glint of humor in the general's eyes and sensed a new respect in Jackson's manner. From then on, the two were friends.

Not long after that, General Jackson moved his headquarters to a plantation just upriver from the one where the British troops were quartered. Both were on the east bank of the Mississippi. Jackson began to prepare a battle line along an old canal bed that ran at right angles to the Mississippi and separated the two plantations. The canal ran eastward to a large swampy area.

Every man was put to work at piling up a dirt wall, with spaces left open for cannon placement. Someone thought the many bales of cotton, awaiting shipment on the levee in New Orleans, would make a good barricade. A few were brought down and stacked. It wasn't long, however, before one caught fire when a cannon went off. It smoked so badly that the men were blinded until the smoldering fire was put out. The officers realized that the cotton bales would be a disaster in battle. Building the wall with logs and mud took longer, but the bales were set aside.

Tension built as rumors spread of more troops arriving at the British plantation camp. Fortunately, more volunteers also arrived to aid in the defense of New Orleans. Many were from Jackson's home state of Tennessee, from Kentucky, and from Mississippi.

On January 3, Shreve was called to General Jackson's plantation headquarters. He went into the living room that served as an office and found Jackson with a large map spread out on a table.

"Look here, Shreve," Jackson said, pointing to a place on the map downriver. "Fort St. Philip. You've been there." He moved his pencil upriver toward the British-held area. "British guns guarding the river are here."

"Yes, sir."

"Now, sir, I am beginning to realize that you are a man who always does what he sets out to do. Do you think you might, with your steamboat, pass those British guns and get down to Fort St. Philip with supplies?"

Shreve studied the map, noting the width and channel markings of the river, the sandbars, and the islands. "I can, sir," he said, "if I may choose when to do it and have a little time to get the steamboat ready."

"How much time do you need?"

"Twenty-four hours, maybe less. Can you have the supplies put on board the *Enterprise* this afternoon?"

"Yes," the general said. After a moment's thought, Shreve requested the use of some cotton bales, bale hooks, and rope.

He had a busy day. To protect the *Enterprise* from cannon fire, he ordered thick bales of cotton hung over the sides with ropes and iron hooks. Then he assembled his crew to tell them the plan.

"We have to slip by the British guns as silently as possible. Keep the fires low—no tell-tale sparks can fly from the stack. We'll have to use keelboat methods when we cut the engine, so have your poles handy."

After the loading was completed, the *Enterprise* was moved downriver a short distance to a position just above headquarters.

The captain called his crew together once more. "Is there anyone among you who wants to stay here? If so, now's the time to leave."

The men looked from one to another, each aware of the great risks involved in trying to slip past the British guns, deliver the supplies to Fort St. Philip, and then, at even greater risk, bring the *Enterprise* back up the Mississippi.

No one spoke.

"Are you all with me?"

"Aye, Captain," they said, and not a man turned away.

As darkness came, fog began to settle over the river.

"Excellent," Captain Shreve told John. "We start at midnight. Tell the men to get some rest."

At eleven-thirty, the *Enterprise*'s firemen began their work. By midnight, steam pressure was up and all was in readiness. The fog was so thick that Shreve could scarcely see the river ahead as he took his place in the pilot house.

The paddle wheel began to turn and the *Enterprise*, running in total darkness, eased away from the landing. Slowly she moved downriver until Shreve guessed they were not far from the British guns. He passed the word to shut down the engine and be ready to use poles.

There was only the sound of water lapping against the boat and a slight hiss from the boilers as the *Enterprise* moved along at a speed hardly above that of the river current. Captain Shreve had memorized the navigational hazards on this stretch of the river, but in the fog his moves had to be made with great caution.

"We're passing the guns now," he said in a low voice to John, who stood beside him in the pilot house. "Go below and tell the men to keep poling while we go through the English Turn." The English Turn was a horseshoe bend in the river just below the position of the British guns.

Slowly, almost silently, the steamboat slipped along. Not one British gun was fired. The men lifted and set the poles with scarcely a ruffling of the misted waters, and the fog helped muffle whatever sounds the boat made. John returned to the pilot house.

"Tell the crew to be ready for low steam power when we round the bend," Shreve said with a sigh of relief. "Looks as if we made it!"

As a new day dawned, gray and foggy, the *Enterprise* eased into a mooring close to Fort St. Philip. Soon a group of surprised soldiers were unloading the supplies, which included a thirty-two pounder—a cannon larger than any they already had. With it and the other ammunition the *Enterprise* had brought, the fort had a much better chance of stopping any enemy ships that might try to make their way up the Mississippi.

All day the crew of the *Enterprise* rested, knowing that the real trial was still ahead of them. At day's end, Shreve spoke to them.

"Last night, the fog muffled both the sight and sound of us and we got through. But you can be very sure that by now the British know we are here. They'll be watching for us tonight. Since we're going upriver, we'll have to use steam power all the way. We'll keep our engine low as we draw near, but they're sure to hear us coming. The plan is to open her up full speed when we draw into range of the guns—and hope and pray that we get through!"

Shreve paused a moment, looking at each of his men. "Are you all still with me?"

They answered as one. "Aye, Captain."

Good fortune brought fog once again to help them, but as the *Enterprise* approached the British camp, a guard on duty sent word that he could hear a steamboat coming. Though muffled by the fog, the clanking and hissing sounds reached him.

The British guns fired.

"Full speed ahead!" Shreve called out and moved the boat as far from the eastern bank as he could without hanging up in mud or on a sandbar. The crew did all it could to keep the *Enterprise* moving as fast as possible, even though the men were close enough to see the bright flashes of gun and cannon fire. The sounds were drowned out by the noises of the steamboat as the paddle wheel churned water and the gears and connecting rods groaned and clanked in the hold.

The *Enterprise* shook as if it were about to fall apart, and the crew could scarcely tell when gunfire hit the bales of cotton. It was soon clear, however, that the British were baffled by the steamboat, a new target for them. The cotton bales protected the boat's wooden sides from the few well-aimed shots, and the rest sputtered into the water. She made it through unharmed.

As they eased into the New Orleans landing, Shreve joined his crew in a loud cheer.

"We showed 'em, didn't we, Cap'n?" one of the boatmen called out.

Shreve grinned. "You sure did, boys. I'm right proud of every one of you."

This time when he walked into Jackson's headquarters he didn't wait for an aide to announce him. He went into the general's office and told him of the safe return of the *Enterprise* after the successful completion of her assigned duty.

"I didn't think you could do it, Captain," Jackson said. "I am sure this is the first time a steamboat has ever run a blockade." He stood to shake hands. "I am eternally grateful to you, Shreve."

Three

THE attack on New Orleans was expected at any hour. Jackson's soldiers, encamped behind the finished defense wall, could scarcely sleep for they knew that the call to action could come at any moment.

There were no more missions for the *Enterprise*, and Captain Shreve, with nothing to do, felt restless. He was sure he could be useful in the battle line, for he had learned to handle a rifle as a boy helping to get meat for his family's table. On the morning of January 7, he went to see General Jackson.

"General, I'm reporting for duty as a Pennsylvania sharpshooter," he said. Jackson welcomed Shreve to the land forces—until such time as his services with the *Enterprise* would be needed again. He assigned Shreve to the defense line, manning a twenty-four pound gun at the end of the wall nearest the river.

Jackson's army was a strange and assorted lot of men. Some were in the United States Army and wore a uniform of buff trousers and a dark blue coat. Others were from state militia companies, called to duty when there was an emergency. Some of these, such as the Louisiana militiamen, wore uniforms, but many had come from the frontier. They wore their buckskins or their home-made clothes of linsey-woolsey.

General Jackson was awake long before the mist-ridden dawn of January 8, 1815. So were most of his men, for word had come at two A.M. that the British had been seen forming their battle lines.

Of his approximately six thousand men, Jackson had about four thousand behind the defense wall; the others placed where surprise attacks might come. The British forces were said to be larger, with some eight thousand fighting men. At five A.M., Jackson's scouts reported that an estimated force of more than five thousand British was advancing toward the mud and log wall. The Battle of New Orleans had begun.

The British rushed the wall, but the defenders held their fire. One British officer, as he reached the top of the wall, boldly called out, "Surrender, you Yankee rascals!"

"Fire!" came the American order at last. The officer, along with many British soldiers, fell to the ground. The Yankee rascals brought down wave after wave of charging men.

In a few hours the battle was over, with about two thousand six hundred British soldiers killed, wounded, or missing. Of the American defenders, only seven men were killed and six severely wounded. The city of New Orleans had not been touched.

The British retreated to plan their next move. Jackson needed Captain Shreve and the *Enterprise* again, to reposition some of the American troops and to take supplies where they might be needed. With the former British gun positions no longer active, the *Enterprise* made another trip down the river to Fort St. Philip to deliver fuses for the fort's largest cannons. British sailing ships were entering the river from the Gulf and only with these big guns could the men stop them. The delivery of the fuses was made in time and, on January 18, the British ships could not pass the fort and withdrew to the Gulf.

There were other skirmishes here and there, but on February 13, a messenger arrived carrying important news to General Jackson. The War of 1812 had officially ended on

December 24, when a peace treaty had been signed in the city of Ghent, in Belgium. It had taken seven weeks for the news to come by sailing ship across the Atlantic and the Gulf of Mexico to New Orleans. The Battle of New Orleans soon became known as "the needless battle," for it was fought two weeks after the war was officially over. However, no one argued that it had been a *useless* battle, for it won new respect for the American military forces.

The *Enterprise*'s work for the United States Army had not yet ended. There were prisoners to be delivered to the British near the mouth of the Mississippi and exchanged for Americans to be brought to New Orleans. Men and supplies were moved to army posts, and the people who had been taken upriver for safety were brought home. Through most of this, the *Enterprise* was the only steamboat in service, for the *Vesuvius* remained immovable until early March.

Jackson sent the *Enterprise* up the Red River to return soldiers and supplies to Fort St. Denis, in central Louisiana. It was while he was there that Captain Shreve learned of the Red River's biggest problem. His steamboat could not go any farther. The way was blocked by an enormous collection of driftwood, nearly two hundred miles long, known as the Great Raft of the Red River. The Raft was so old that new trees were growing in rotted driftwood, making it look like an island. Only small keelboats could make their way around it to go farther.

Seeing this, Shreve felt certain there was some way this great mass of driftwood could be removed. The Red must be opened to steamboats. The Raft not only blocked transportation, but also caused the river to spread out and flood land that could otherwise be farmed. Along the river now there were mostly swampland and stagnant bayous, home to alligators, snakes, muskrats, and countless insects that carried disease. Shreve thought a great deal about that blockade in the river as he headed back to New Orleans.

On March 12, 1815, martial law was finally lifted and the *Enterprise*'s work for General Jackson completed. Captain

Shreve was called to headquarters for the last time. As the two men shook hands, Jackson said, "All I heard about you was right, Captain. When you set about to do something, you get it done. I expect to hear more of you in the years ahead."

"And I of you, General." Both men were right, for when Andrew Jackson became President of the United States in 1829, one of his acts was to renew a government appointment for Captain Henry Miller Shreve, who was by then in charge of clearing the rivers of snags, making them safer for steamboats.

But that was far in the future as Captain Shreve left Jackson's headquarters and returned to the *Enterprise*. For now, he was considering how he could get his boat back to Brownsville, Pennsylvania. He wanted to start upriver immediately, for he had word that his third child was soon to be born. He also needed to carry freight to pay the costs of the voyage back up the rivers. But two problems stood in the way of loading the *Enterprise* and starting for home.

One was that the Fulton-Livingston men would surely try to stop him from leaving with freight and passengers on board. By state law, their company had exclusive rights to the use of steam power in the waters of Louisiana. They could have him arrested for using his steamboat. They could even have the *Enterprise* taken from him if he tried to take a load of freight upriver.

Captain Shreve, however, strongly believed that he and anyone else had a right to trade in New Orleans, or along the rivers. This Louisiana law that gave rights only to certain people was against his ideas of freedom and equality. So he was planning to break the law, hoping he could prove it unconstitutional in court. He planned to do this even though he knew he would have a fight on his hands—a fight that he couldn't afford to lose. Fortunately, Shreve was well-prepared. Before he had left New Orleans with his keelboat in the summer of 1814, he had hired a lawyer to help him.

Now, almost a year later, Shreve recalled that steaming hot July day when he had gone to see if Abner Duncan, a New

Orleans attorney, would work for him against the powerful Fulton-Livingston Company. As Shreve entered Duncan's office, the lawyer—a stocky man in his shirt-sleeves—had been seated at a large desk covered with piles of paper. Wiping his brow with a kerchief, Duncan had risen to greet his visitor and then removed a stack of books from a chair so Shreve could sit down. The two were not strangers, as Captain Shreve had called on Mr. Duncan for some minor legal matters in the past.

Shreve told Duncan of his plans to bring a non-Fulton steamboat to New Orleans very soon, and that he intended to take it back upriver with cargo, and even a few passengers. He still remembered Duncan's astonishment.

"You what?" Duncan had cried out and jumped to his feet faster than Shreve thought the heavy man could move. Then, as if worn out, he had taken his seat again and reached for the mahogany box that held his cigars. He had offered one to Shreve, who refused. Then with great deliberation, Duncan had cut off the tip of a cigar and lighted it from a little oil lamp on his desk. After several strong pulls, he finally had the cigar burning and blew out a puff of smoke. Leaning back and putting his feet on the desk, he had asked, "Do you realize what you're getting into?"

Shreve had tried to stay calm, and replied, "The Mississippi River doesn't belong to Louisiana. Any man smart enough to get a steamboat down the river should be allowed to trade here."

"Take it easy, Henry," Duncan had said, sensing Shreve's anger, "or you won't live long enough to run a steamboat anywhere!"

They had talked quite a while. Shreve learned that Duncan, too, felt the exclusive rights law was undemocratic—maybe even unconstitutional—and that he'd enjoy pitting his legal skills against those of the Fulton-Livingston lawyers. Before leaving the office, Shreve had paid Duncan five hundred dollars as a retainer and promised to pay another fifteen hundred when Duncan won his case. Certain that a lawsuit would be filed when Captain Shreve brought a steamboat to New Orleans, Duncan had begun planning how to fight it.

Today Shreve would sit down again with his lawyer. Duncan was in his office as usual, leaning back with his feet on the desk, a big cigar in his hand, when Henry walked in.

"Well, Henry! You really are the hero around here!" Duncan said. He took his feet from the desk and let the front legs of his chair return to the floor. "Everyone's been talking about how you and the *Enterprise* helped save our city."

Once again he cleared papers and law books from a chair.

"Thanks, Abner. But I'll bet there are a few people who aren't joining in singing my praises! The Fulton-Livingston lawyers, for example."

"You may be right about that, Henry. In fact, I'm sure you are."

"Oh? Is it that bad? I thought perhaps, since Fulton's death, that exclusive rights law might not still be in force. You did read about Robert Fulton dying, didn't you?"

"Yes. I saw an item in the *Gazette*. But no, Henry," Duncan said. "The law still stands, for the rights go to the heirs of Fulton and Livingston."

"Do you think their attorneys will let me load up the *Enterprise* and leave?"

"Not on your life, Henry! No chance at all, unless you give in and pay their license fee."

"I was afraid of that. Well, when I'm ready to go, I'm going to advertise for freight and passengers, just as if that exclusive rights law wasn't on the books. What do you think will happen?"

"Edward Livingston—he's representing the company—will have you served with papers to try to hold your boat in port, at least until you unload all the freight and give your passengers their money back."

"Edward Livingston? Isn't he Robert Livingston's brother? I must say he doesn't know me very well. I'll not unload. I'm counting on you to be ready with some legal work, too, Ab."

"He's Robert's brother, all right. And keep in mind that he has big plans to take over all the shipping again. The *Vesuvius* is advertising right now for the Natchez trade. I'm told the *Aetna* is about ready to come down from Pittsburgh. They're real sure that this time they have a boat that can handle the rough waters between Natchez and Shippingport."

"I doubt it," Shreve said.

"Well, I don't know a thing about steamboats, but that's the plan they've worked out. The *Vesuvius* will do as the *New Orleans* did and run between here and Natchez. The *Aetna* will pick up passengers and freight there. And when she gets to Shippingport, they'll have a smaller boat ready to make the Louisville to Pittsburgh run. Yes, Henry, they've got it all figured out—and they're not going to let you interfere if they can help it."

Shreve was up and pacing. "I hoped maybe they wouldn't bother me. But I guess that was too good to be true. Well, what's our plan?"

"Sit down, Henry. I've got a lot to tell you."

Shreve sat down. "You haven't changed your mind about helping me, have you?"

Duncan laughed. "Well, I was sure tempted, Henry. They made me a good offer. As soon as he heard you were coming to New Orleans with a steamboat, Edward Livingston came marching in here. He wanted to buy me off. He offered me three thousand dollars to give up your case. What do you think of that, young man?"

Shreve was on his feet again. "You know what I think, Abner? I think they're running scared! They know I have a better steamboat than theirs—and what's more they know that the law giving them exclusive rights won't stand up in court."

Duncan lit the cigar he had been holding. "That's your opinion, Henry, but it may not be the judge's." He blew out a puff of smoke.

Pounding the desk, Shreve said, "Any judge who thinks that's a good law shouldn't be in a court room. Why, look what it does to our country! The Fulton boats aren't strong enough to do the job they're supposed to do, so all the people up the rivers have to do without the things they need."

Shreve was tense with anger. Duncan said nothing, waiting for him to calm down. Finally, his voice quieter, Shreve said, "The Livingstons are like the dog in the manger. Remember that story, Ab? The dog didn't like the oats in the manger but he wouldn't let the horses who did like them get to them. I say if they can't build a good steamboat, they should let someone who can take over."

There was silence a moment, and then Duncan said quietly, "Don't you want to know what I told Edward Livingston?"

Shreve smiled. "Of course I do. Sorry, Abner. Do I still have an attorney?"

"Well, Livingston's hired every lawyer in the city to work with him. Except one."

"You, I hope."

Duncan blew out another puff of smoke. "Yes, me. And I often wonder if I have good sense!" He looked down at his cigar and knocked the ashes off onto the floor. Then he went on, "But you know, young man, the more I learn of Livingston's ways of working, the surer I am that I should fight for you—and that we'll win in the long run. But it won't be easy."

"But if the judge decides in our favor? What then?"

"They'll appeal—you can count on that. And the law still stands while we wait for another court hearing. They'll fight it all the way through the court system."

Shreve was calmer now. "What happens when I load up and get ready to take the *Enterprise* back, Abner?" he asked.

"They'll serve you with papers to stop you, and you get in touch with me immediately. When do you plan to embark?"

"Not until the river rises with the spring floods."

"Why do you have to wait that long?"

"Well, Abner, I'm going to tell you something in confidence, something I don't want Edward Livingston to hear.

You know I've been up to Natchez several times with the *Enterprise*. The last time I was there, I tried the currents just upriver. If I'd had freight on board, I couldn't have made it. When I leave here, it's going to be with a pay load—and I've got to make it all the way to Pittsburgh."

"How do you plan to do that?"

"When the water rises I can choose an easier route than when the water is low. I'll get that steamboat home, all right. But don't look for me to bring the *Enterprise* back down here."

Duncan looked startled. "You mean you're going to give up? You're going to quit steamboating?"

"Not on your life! As soon as I get home I'm going to start over. I have ideas I *know* will work. I'm going to build a better engine and a better boat, one that will master anything the Mississippi puts in her way!"

Four

DURING the next few weeks, Captain Shreve could scarcely conceal his impatience as he watched the *Vesuvius* load up and leave for Natchez, return and load again. He would have liked to be on his way upriver, too, earning money with cargo and passengers on the *Enterprise*, but he didn't want to defy the Fulton-Livingston monopoly until he was ready to go all the way home. While he waited for the river to deepen, the *Enterprise* remained at the landing. Shreve and his crew went over every inch of the boat, putting it in top condition.

Then on April 24, the new Fulton boat, the *Aetna*, came chugging down the river to New Orleans. The crew brought good news—the rivers were rising at last, even overflowing the banks farther to the north. Captain Shreve set his departure date for May 6 and advertised in the *Gazette* for freight and passengers.

The morning of May 6, the *Enterprise* was ready. On board were barrels of sugar and molasses and bales of cotton. Twelve men and two women were in the passenger cabins, and Shreve's crew awaited orders. All the wood that could be carried stood ready to keep the fires going.

"Fire up," Captain Shreve ordered. He went out on the

deck, wondering how soon a law officer would show up. He didn't have long to wait. A man came striding along the levee and boldly walked down the gangplank onto the boat.

"Can't leave with any cargo, Captain Shreve," the New Orleans law officer said as he held out papers to Shreve. "Law states that you must have a license from Fulton and Livingston."

Showing no surprise, Captain Shreve accepted the papers. "Keep the steam up when ready!" he called back to his mate. "And tell the passengers not to leave—there's just a short delay."

Following the law officer up the gangplank, Shreve hurried to Duncan's home. The lawyer was just about to have breakfast.

"Sit down and have a cup of coffee, Henry. You'll be on your way within an hour."

Duncan already had the necessary papers drawn up and bail payment arranged. The Fulton-Livingston men didn't even realize Shreve was leaving until the *Enterprise* was on the river and headed north. Duncan would take care of the court appearances in Shreve's absence.

The steamboat made her way with little difficulty as far as Natchez. Continuing upriver from there, she struggled against the currents, as Captain Shreve had known she would. He handled the problem as he had planned, moving onto flooded fields where the current was less strong.

Convinced that the *Enterprise*'s engine was little better than the Fulton low-pressure steam engines, Shreve knew he needed an engine powerful enough to move a large boat with a paying load of freight. At night in his cabin, he worked on drawings of a high-pressure engine, based on those he had seen in Pittsburgh. As he sketched and planned, he could hardly wait to get home and begin construction.

Twenty-five days after departing from New Orleans, the *Enterprise* tied up at Shippingport, Kentucky, just below the Falls of the Ohio. The *Enterprise* was the first steamboat to

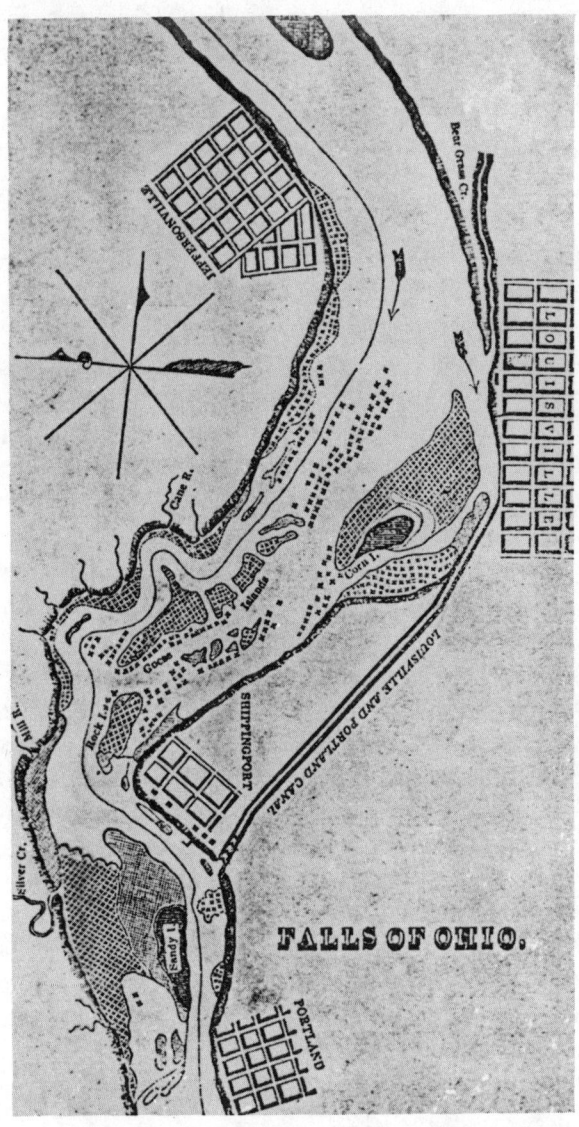

This map shows the Falls of the Ohio after 1830, when the Louisville and Portland Canal was completed. Dangerous rocks are shown as x's.

attempt the upstream passage of the Falls, for none of the other steamboats had ever come back this far. Everyone wondered if she could go up the Falls under steam power alone.

The pilot who came on board the *Enterprise* was hopeful. "Let's try her under her own power, Captain."

"Off the record," Shreve said quietly, "I don't think she can do it. But we'll try."

He was right. The current was too strong, and the men had to use a method called warping that Shreve had often used to move his keelboat under certain conditions. To warp, men in a rowboat took a rope attached to the steamboat's prow to an island or shore where stout trees grew. The rope was wrapped around a tree trunk, and the men on the steamboat hauled in the rope to move the steamboat forward. Then the rope was moved to a tree farther ahead, and the process repeated.

As the *Enterprise* moved smoothly toward the Louisville landing, the pilot, standing alongside Shreve at the big wheel, asked if Fulton's *Aetna* had reached New Orleans.

"Yes, she made it fine," Captain Shreve said.

"Well, I hope they never ask us to get that steamboat back over the Falls. What a time we had getting her over them going *with* the current! We were just lucky, I guess. That *Aetna* needs more water to float her than we ever have here— we just had to trust to luck and shoot her through at full power. We scraped some rocks, and we were scared we'd wrecked her."

The pilot paused a moment. Then he asked, "Are you coming back soon with this steamboat, Captain Shreve? She's a pretty fine boat, seems to me."

"No, I'm going to build a new steamboat." Shreve laughed. "One like you've never seen before! I won't be back this way until next year when she's finished. But be ready for a surprise when you see me again!"

Shreve was in for a surprise himself. A crowd had gathered as he was docking the *Enterprise*, and now the people cheered loudly. Many wanted to shake his hand as he came ashore. He was the first to bring a steamboat all the way up the Mississippi and Ohio rivers to Louisville, something they had hoped would happen ever since the *New Orleans* had headed downriver in December of 1811.

In addition, Captain Shreve was greeted as a war hero because of his successful run past the British guns to aid the men at Fort St. Philip. A special dinner had been planned in his honor.

At the dinner, Shreve's twenty-five-day voyage from New Orleans was the main subject of conversation. It seemed truly marvelous, for three months was the usual time. Everyone seemed sure that the steamboat had finally mastered the Mississippi—everyone but Shreve.

"Speech! Speech!" the dinner guests called out. Shreve rose to his feet, not quite sure what to say. These people took the return of the *Enterprise* as an indication that they would now have regular steamboat service from New Orleans. Shreve knew that time had not yet come. He doubted if the *Aetna* would do as well as the *Enterprise*. After speaking very briefly, he closed with, "I thank you for your welcome and your praise, and I hope to be much more deserving of it in the years ahead."

A letter from his wife, Mary, was awaiting him at the Louisville post office. Their son, Hampden Zane Shreve, had been born on April 8. Mary and their two little girls, Rebecca and Harriet, had heard the news that the steamboat was a success and would be watching for its return to Brownsville.

On July 10, after unloading its freight at Pittsburgh, Shreve docked his boat at Brownsville. The actual traveling time for the upriver journey from New Orleans to Pittsburgh was thirty-four days. The *Enterprise* was considered the marvel of the century.

Captain Shreve, after meeting his new son and getting reacquainted with his family, was soon at work completing his drawings and plans for the new boat he wanted to build. One morning he went to show them to Daniel French.

"Are you ready to make another run to New Orleans on the *Enterprise?*" French asked.

"Dan, I wouldn't advise anyone to take her farther than Louisville. If it hadn't been for the flood waters, I don't think I'd have made it back here." Shreve paused, tapping his roll of drawings on the desk. "No, I'm turning her over to you to get a new master. I want a steamboat with a high-pressure engine."

French looked up in surprise. "What do you mean, Henry? My engines have higher pressure than the Fulton engines."

"Forty or fifty pounds isn't enough, Dan!" Shreve said, impatiently. "I want an engine like the Evans engines that build up to one hundred pounds of pressure."

French shook his head. "No, Henry. I'm afraid the boiler can't take that much pressure. It would blow up!"

"The one in the flour mill at Pittsburgh has been working just fine for years," Shreve shot back. "They've had no explosions there or anywhere else where a true, high-pressure engine has been used."

"But no one has used one on a steamboat."

"Oliver Evans is sure it would work, Dan, and he's been making high-pressure engines for years. Of course you'd have to use safety valves to let out steam when the pressure gets too high."

When French did not answer, Shreve started to unroll his drawings. "How about building a high-pressure engine here for me, Dan?" he asked.

French shook his head. "I'm afraid of high pressure, Henry."

"Well, I'm not. If Oliver Evans has faith in high-pressure engines, so do I!"

Shreve paused, looking at French perched on a high stool at his work table.

"But, Henry, why take the risk?"

"Why, Dan? Because we need a steamboat that will come back upriver without the help of floodwaters, that's why!" Shreve rolled his papers up.

"A well-built, high-pressure engine's as safe as any low-pressure engine. Safer, in fact, because you're less likely to force it to work up more pressure than it should. I've heard the masters of the Fulton boats block the safety valve so they can get up more power—now that's *really* dangerous!"

Shreve's voice had risen as he talked. "Well, Dan? Should I show you my plans?"

There was silence for a moment. Then French said, "Henry, I just can't go along with you. Why don't we wait and see how the *Dispatch* does the job? She'll be ready as soon as the ice breaks next spring."

"Is she bigger than the *Enterprise?*"

"No. She's a bit smaller."

"That won't do—can't carry enough pay load. I can't wait, Dan. If our company doesn't want to build a boat from my plans, I'll sell out my shares and form a new company that is willing to try my ideas."

And that is what Henry Shreve did. He began to look for four others who were willing to buy shares in a steamboat building company, for the law required five to form a corporation. He went to see his old friends, Robert Clark and Neal Gillespie, who had built a keelboat for him. The idea of a high-pressure steam engine didn't seem to bother them, so he spread out his drawings for them to see.

Clark and Gillespie studied the plans with interest, but after they had seen the details of Shreve's boat, there was silence. Then Gillespie said, "Are you serious about this, Henry? This boat looks ridiculous! Why do you want a second deck stuck up there? It's top-heavy!"

"Now hold on!" Shreve told them. "As you can see, I've put the boilers on the main deck. That's much more practical than having them down in the hold—you can have the wood stacked right at hand with less labor."

"That part makes sense," Gillespie admitted.

Shreve pointed out more features. "I've got some of the machinery down in the hold, just as it is on other steamboats. But I believe most of the hold should be used for freight, so I've put the passenger cabins on an extra deck above the main one. You have to have plenty of room for passengers—that's how you make money. So we need a second deck."

"Hm-m-mm," Clark said as he studied the drawings. "I never saw a steam engine like this one, either. You've got the cylinders in a horizontal position. An engine for a steamboat always stands upright."

"Who decided all that?" Henry asked. "Just because that's what has been done so far doesn't mean it's the best way to design one. If you really study these plans, you'll see that the engine will work. I know it will. And it takes up less space and weighs much less than any engine in a Fulton boat, or even Dan French's."

"But you have side paddle wheels like the Fulton boats. Why not a stern wheel like the *Enterprise* has?"

"I believe you can get more drive and have easier handling with side wheels. There are shorter connections to run from the engine."

The boat builders looked at each other. Clark finally spoke. "Shreve, you've always had a good head on your shoulders. But somehow you've gone too far this time. I don't think we want to build this crazy boat. When people see it, they'll think we've gone berserk! We'll be the laughingstock of Brownsville."

Shreve gathered up his drawings. "All right, boys, if that's the way you feel. But you know what they say—he who laughs last, laughs best. I'll find a builder who doesn't think my boat is a joke."

He walked away. That evening, at home, he looked over his plans and drawings. Carefully, he checked every detail.

When he rolled them up again and rose from his chair, he said aloud, "It's a good design and it will work. Somewhere, there are people who will see how important it is to build this boat! I'll find them."

"I'll be gone about five days, Mary, if the weather stays fine," Captain Shreve told his wife several days later. "But don't worry if I'm delayed. I may have to stay longer to get this job done."

He had spent two more days talking to boat builders and possible investors around Brownsville, with no success. Now he was going to Wheeling, which at that time was in Virginia, on the Ohio River. It was a journey of about forty miles by land, and Mary had packed changes of clothing and a razor into Shreve's saddlebags.

Shreve walked the two blocks down Front Street to the livery stable. A riding horse was soon saddled and ready for him, and he rode down to the ferry landing to cross the Monongahela River.

He would follow the new National Road, the first government highway in the United States, all the way to Wheeling.

The National Road was still little more than a narrow cleared trail, for work from the Mon to Wheeling had just begun in that year of 1815. Shreve stopped at a little wayside inn that night and continued on toward Wheeling the next morning.

He knew many people in Wheeling, for he had often stopped there on his trading voyages with his keelboats.

When he reached the village, he followed the road as it sloped down toward the Ohio and the mouth of Wheeling Creek. At the foot of the slope, on the banks of Wheeling Creek, was the boatyard of George White. George was the man Henry Shreve wanted to talk to.

White was there and held out a hand in welcome.

"Captain Shreve! I've been reading about you in the newspapers. My friend Noah Lane and I were talking about you just a day or two ago. We want advice on how to build a steamboat, and it seems like you're the man to give it."

Shreve was pleased. "That's good news, because I've come here with plans for one. I'm looking for investors and for someone to build the hull and do the carpentry work."

Soon the two were huddled over the drawings. The boat was to be one hundred and forty feet long and twenty-five feet wide—a long boat, but not as wide as the Fulton steamboats.

Its basic shape was that of a large keelboat, except for a second deck that reached back to the stern. A gentlemen's passenger cabin was forward in this upper space, with a ladies' cabin aft.

Shreve watched to see White's reactions as he explained the new features of his boat and its engine. George White did not laugh.

"It makes sense to me, Captain," he said. "The double deck may look a bit odd, but it adds a lot of space that will help the boat earn money for us. It looks a bit top-heavy, but with most of the weight below deck, it won't tip over—as long as it stays on the rivers. I wouldn't want to take it out on the ocean."

"Then you'll build it for me? Part of your payment will be a one-fifth ownership of the boat."

"I'll be honored to build your steamboat, Captain Shreve. Let me go and get Noah. I'll bet he'll be interested, too."

Mr. Lane, a well-dressed older gentleman, soon joined them, and the three talked a long time. Lane was interested in investing in a steamboat and had questions about the safety of the high-pressure engine. Henry explained its operation. Then he took out a newspaper in which a letter was printed.

"This is what the inventor Oliver Evans has to say about a high-pressure engine in a steamboat," Shreve said, and he began to read aloud. "'I believe my principle is the only one suitable for propelling boats up the Mississippi.'"

Lane and White took the paper to read the rest of the article for themselves. When they had finished, Captain Shreve said, "After seeing the low-pressure steamboats struggling against Mississippi River currents down in Louisiana, I completely agree with Oliver Evans. My own design is not a copy of Mr. Evans's high-pressure engines, but it works on the same principles."

"What about the safety factor?" Lane asked.

Henry made a sketch of how the safety valves would be placed on the cylinder ends where steam pressure built up, and how they would open to let steam out when the pressure was building too high. There was a weighted arm that would tilt to hold the valve open until the pressure was lowered.

"It's actually safer than a low-pressure engine," he said. "Low pressure means less power, and when a boat needs more power to move against the currents, the engineers on the boat have to risk explosions by blocking the safety valve. More pressure is built up than the boilers and cylinders were designed for, and you have a real danger of explosion."

"I can understand that," Mr. Lane said.

Turning back to his drawings, Shreve said, "My engine has almost five times the power built into it that the *New Orleans* had. With all that power, I don't think there would ever be the need for more—or the temptation to block the safety valve."

Mr. Lane was satisfied. He agreed to buy a one-fifth share, and George White agreed to another share in return for some of the material plus labor. The work would begin as soon as possible.

"There are still some of those old timbers from the ruins of Fort Henry, Captain," White said. "They would be great for this boat, and the town wants them cleared away. We'll get the woodcutters busy for the rest of what we need."

Henry remembered another matter to discuss with his investors. "I'm still fighting the Fulton-Livingston monopoly, gentlemen. It is highly likely that when this steamboat goes down to New Orleans, they'll try to seize it."

Lane spoke up. "Captain Shreve, even more than your work in aiding Jackson in his victory, and even more than your bringing the first steamboat up the rivers, I admire your courage. For a young man with nothing more than what he has made for himself, I think it is remarkable that you stand up to the wealthy men of the East who try to control our development here in the West. I will back you all the way."

A glow of warmth still hung over Henry as he saddled up to go home. Excitement grew within him. He was confident now, with White and Lane backing him, that he would find two more investors. At last, the steamboat he *knew* would work was about to be built!

Five

WHEN her husband arrived at home, Mary Shreve told him that Robert Clark and Neal Gillespie had been there that morning. They had seemed very anxious to talk with Shreve as soon as he returned.

When he stopped by to see them the next day, he had a surprise waiting for him. "We think we were a mite hasty the other day, Shreve." Clark said. "We'll build your new steamboat."

Shreve said nothing for a moment, looking at his two old friends. "Even if you'll be the laughingstock of Brownsville?" he asked.

"We'll take a chance on that!" Clark said, smiling.

"What made you change your mind?"

"Well, to be honest about it, we figured we were passin' up a chance to make some money," Gillespie admitted. "You've been right on just about everything you've ever tried since we first met you years ago, Henry, and you know more about steamboats and the rivers than anyone else. So we decided most likely we'd be sorry we turned you down."

"That's good to hear," Shreve said. "But you're too late. George White down in Wheeling is building my steamboat. He's most likely got the keel cut and set in the cradle by now."

There was silence for a moment. Then he added, "But if you really believe in it, I need two more shareholders."

Clark and Gillespie looked at each other. Gillespie nodded, and Clark said, "Sold!"

When the papers were drawn up and signed, Shreve had the financial backing he needed. He later learned that the keel had been laid, as White had planned, using the well-seasoned timbers from old Fort Henry, and woodcutters were working in the forest near the White boatyards to cut trees for the decking, cabins, and other parts of the boat.

Now he could get started on building his steam engine and other machinery. Confidently, he bought a building lot across the street from his home on Front Street and put up a machine shop. From foundries and factories in Pittsburgh and Brownsville, he ordered the iron castings and other metal parts he needed for his engine.

Brownsville was home to several "old-timers" in the boat building and operating businesses, and these and other people with time to spare often came to see what was going on in Shreve's shop. As the operating machinery took shape, it was obvious to onlookers that it was completely different from the power assembly in any low-pressure steamboat. Some delighted in finding fault. One old fellow who had been a riverboatman and thought he knew all there was to know said, "What in tarnation are you doin' there, Henry Shreve? There ain't never been no boat run with an engine like that'un! Why don't you let Dan French tell you how to fix it so's it'll work?"

They would make little jokes and wink at each other. Shreve let it all go by him like so many leaves blowing by on those late autumn days. He knew he had the respect of the people who mattered to him. He also was convinced of the soundness of his designs and ideas.

Henry Shreve turned thirty years old that October of 1815. He worked most of the time in his shop, but now and then took a week off for a trip to Wheeling. The hull had been completed, caulked, and painted, and was launched on the

Ohio River at the mouth of Wheeling Creek. The building of the decks and cabins was proceeding.

Back in his shop, Shreve continued his grinding, drilling, and setting of bolts during the winter months. He had the blacksmith make pieces to order as he needed them. Finally, his high-pressure engine and the machinery to turn the paddle wheels were put together. The boilers and the cylinders were tested in the workshop. Shreve went over and over the assembly until he felt it was right.

Later, when the steamboat was finished, newspapers reported that the engine was "entirely new and the invention of Captain Shreve." Among its new features was the use of two boilers instead of one, and the placement of these on the deck instead of down in the hold. Each boiler had a smokestack, so Shreve's steamboat was the first to have the tall, double stacks that appeared on all later river steamboats.

When early spring came, Shreve was ready to move his engine to Wheeling. He hauled it down the steep hill at the foot of Front Street by wagon and put it on board a flatboat waiting at the Brownsville waterfront. Before he left home for Wheeling, Henry and Mary had a serious discussion.

Henry explained that in the future, he would be operating his steamboats mostly between New Orleans and Louisville, not able to come back as far as Pittsburgh very often. It seemed only sensible, he said, that they should make their home at Louisville.

He told Mary that it made no sense to bring his new, very large steamboat upriver over the Falls of the Ohio. There would be too many days lost waiting for the water to reach high level. Mary agreed that living near Louisville was a sensible solution, even though it meant moving away from the town that had always been her home. Together they decided that Henry would look for a place to build a new home for the family while on this voyage.

Shreve left then to take his engine to Wheeling. He helped pole the flatboat, as he had done in his early years on the river. The crew got it safely to George White's boatyard, covering a distance of nearly one hundred and fifty miles. There the huge, unfinished steamboat was afloat, tied to its mooring.

After the machinery was moved into place on the steamboat, the workmen began to build the two big paddle wheels, each one sixteen feet in diameter.

There was no more for Shreve to do until the engine could be tested. "While you're working on the wheels, George," he said, "I'm going down to Louisville to arrange for a new home for my family."

"Going down on the *Dispatch*, Captain? I see she's up at the landing."

"Yes, I am. My old friend Israel Gregg is master, and we have a lot to catch up on."

"I heard that Gregg had to come back from New Orleans without any cargo or passengers when he took the *Dispatch* down there in February," White told Shreve.

"I know." Shreve responded. "The Fulton-Livingston men had the marshal order him to leave without cargo or give up the *Dispatch*."

"He's not a fighter like you, Captain, that's plain to see."

Shreve laughed. "Maybe he has more sense than I do, George. And he didn't have my lawyer friend, Abner Duncan, working for him, either." Shreve started to leave, but then turned back. "By the way, George, did I tell you that when my case came up in court, Duncan got a jury trial and won the decision? The jury decided in favor of free and open use of the waters. Most people feel nowadays that's the way it should be."

"Then how could Gregg be forced to leave without cargo?"

"Edward Livingston—he's the attorney for the Fulton-Livingston men—filed an appeal to a higher court. The law stands as long as the case is not settled."

"Doesn't seem right, Captain. But I'm sure that when you get down there with this new boat, you'll find a way to handle it."

"With Duncan's help, George. We're not going to give up.

I'll never let them take this boat from us, no matter what the law says."

Shreve left the boatyard a few minutes later and walked up to the main landing to board the *Dispatch*. This was the only one of Dan French's steamboats still running. After Shreve had left, a young captain had become master of the *Enterprise*. He decided to take the historic steamboat to New Orleans, in spite of Shreve's advice to stay above Louisville. He didn't get very far, for the *Enterprise* was wrecked on the rocks at the lower end of the Falls. The *Dispatch* made the trip to New Orleans, but after Gregg's experience with the Fulton-Livingston men, there had been no more trips down to Louisiana. It now ran between Pittsburgh and Louisville.

Shreve arrived in Louisville just a few days later. It felt good to be traveling under steam power again, and he was thankful that in another month his new boat would be ready.

Exploring the area for a place to live, Shreve found that a new town named Portland was being laid out just below Louisville and Shippingport. A canal around the Falls was in the planning stage and it seemed to Shreve that Portland would be a good place to live. Boat traffic from New Orleans would stop there rather than at Shippingport, once the canal was opened. After buying some property, he made arrangements for the building of a brick home within a block of the riverfront.

Later, back in Wheeling, he found the paddle wheels were in place on the steamboat.

"It's time to give her a name, Captain," George White said. "How about naming her the *Andrew Jackson?*"

Captain Shreve shook his head. "I think highly of General Jackson," he said, "but there's just one name for this steamboat. I want to name her after my childhood hero, George Washington. When I was a boy, my family lived on land Washington had owned, near Brownsville. I lived in the house he had built and learned about machinery in his gristmill. This steamboat's the *Washington*."

Soon the name was painted on the hull and, before long,

almost everyone in Wheeling came down to the waterfront to get a close look at this different kind of steamboat. When the cabins were ready, people walked through them and admired the carpet, curtains, and other furnishings for the passengers. The ladies' and gentlemen's cabins together were about sixty feet long. The men's cabin was about forty feet long, with two rows of curtained bunks, three high along each side. There was room in the center for a dining table. The women were allowed in that room only when the steward told them that a meal was about to be served. They were expected to leave immediately after the meal was finished.

There were a few who considered the *Washington* a strange-looking vessel. "Come a stiff breeze and she'll tip over!" some said. Captain Shreve paid no attention.

When he went home to Brownsville in early May, there was very bad news. Little Hampden Zane Shreve had never been a strong, healthy baby, and now he was very ill. Henry had been home only two days when the baby died. It was a sad family that made preparations soon after for moving to the new home near Louisville. They moved the last week in May.

At last the day came for the *Washington* to have its test run on the Ohio River. Men and women, boys and girls came down to the waterfront to watch. Members of the Ladies' Sewing Circle of Wheeling went to the riverfront for the presentation of a gift they had made—a banner to fly on the steamboat. A small ceremony was to be held just before the test run.

Several members of the sewing circle held the banner out for Captain Shreve to see. They had sewn on it the figure of a woman lying on her side, holding a trumpet in her right hand and an opened scroll of paper in her left.

The leader of the group said, "Captain Shreve, we have pictured the Goddess of Fame, because we feel you deserve all the fame you have already won and will win with this steamboat." Everyone clapped, and then the spokeswoman turned to the group holding the banner and said, "Now, let us show him the reverse side, please."

The women turned the banner and Captain Shreve saw DON'T GIVE UP THE SHIP spelled out in large blue letters. He knew, of course, that these words had become famous during the War of 1812. They were spoken first by James Lawrence, commander of the American frigate *Chesapeake*, as he lay dying on his ship in a battle with a British frigate off the east coast on June 1, 1813. A few months later, the words were put on a banner flown on the *Lawrence*, the flagship of U.S. Commander Oliver Hazard Perry in the victorious Battle of Lake Erie. This victory, in September, 1813, allowed the United States forces to recapture Detroit. Perry became a hero to the American people, especially to the people of the West.

"We were thinking of your battle to make the rivers free to all when we chose those words, Captain Shreve," the spokeswoman explained.

As he accepted the banner, Shreve said, "We'll fly this flag proudly along with the flag of the United States." Then he added, smiling, "If you know me at all, you know that giving up this ship is the last thing I'm likely to do. And now we'll have the test run as soon as steam is up."

He boarded the *Washington* and sounded the hoarse steam horn three times. He had worked out a way to use steam to sound signals. They would be much more easily heard than his trumpet, even if they were not yet as melodious. The ropes were released from the landing, and all was ready.

As soon as the steamboat was clear of the landing, both paddle wheels began to turn. With the sound of the engines and the splashing of the wheels, Captain Shreve could scarcely hear the cheering people watching from the shore, but he could see them waving arms and hats.

The *Washington* picked up speed and went down the Ohio for a few miles, with Captain Shreve in the pilot house. Then he turned her about for the real test. Smoothly and steadily, the big wheels turned and the boat made its way upriver, against the current.

"Pressure test," Shreve ordered, sending the message with John, who had signed on again as his mate.

The crew members built pressure up to the maximum—one hundred pounds on the gauge. Anxiously, Clark, the engineer, watched for the safety valves to open. With a great hissing, steam rushed out, and when the pressure had dropped to a safe level, they closed once more. The *Washington* moved smoothly upriver past the landing at Wheeling before she turned about and returned to the dock.

The cheering was louder than ever as the paddle wheels stopped. The boys waiting on the landing caught the ropes thrown to them from the lower deck and secured the boat.

George White and Noah Lane were among those watching from the shore. They both shook hands with Captain Shreve as he left the steamboat.

"Beautiful!" said White. "Somehow she didn't look top-heavy out there. She seems to sit *on* the water rather than in it—like a swan, in a way. And who ever heard of a swan tipping over?"

The first long voyage of the *Washington* was to begin on Monday, June 3, 1816, at five in the afternoon. She was to go to New Orleans with stops at several cities en route. By half past four that day, it seemed that all of Wheeling had turned out once again to cheer the *Washington* on her way. Freight had been taken on board, and there were twenty-one passengers. Some were going only to the first stop at Marietta, Ohio, but others planned a longer voyage.

Steam was up. The steam horn signaled it was time to leave. As the boat glided away from the landing and the paddle wheels began to turn, a cheer rose from the watchers. The *Washington* moved out into the Ohio, her banner and flag gaily streaming, while the passengers and Captain Shreve waved from the upper deck. Then Shreve went into the pilot house to take over the wheel. He was filled with pride and excitement as the steamboat picked up speed and moved smoothly down the river.

The town of Marietta, the oldest settlement in Ohio, was eighty winding miles away, and the *Washington* made its stop there late on the next afternoon. By that time, Captain

Shreve had discovered some adjustments he wanted to make. He decided to tie up at Marietta while he took care of them. Very late the next afternoon, Wednesday, he moved the boat five miles downriver to Point Harmar, on the Ohio side of the river, and again tied up for the night, after taking on a supply of wood.

Satisfied that his adjustments had been taken care of, he ordered the boilers fired up early the next morning, June 6. The gauge read about ninety pounds pressure when Shreve ordered the cables released, and the *Washington* floated free. The crewmen poled it out into the channel between the Ohio shore and an island, but then it began to drift too fast toward the shallows alongside the island.

"Throw out a kedge!" Captain Shreve called out. A kedge was a light anchor designed to hook into the bottom and hold a boat temporarily. It also could help pull a boat away from a trouble spot. The kedge was thrown out, but before it stopped the boat's drifting, the *Washington* had touched bottom and begun to tilt.

Curious passengers as well as members of the crew had come out on the deck to see what was happening.

"Pole her out, men!" Shreve shouted. The paddle wheels worked together on the same engine, so they could not be started until both were in deeper water.

"Pull in the kedge!"

Several crewmen rushed to the stern deck and pulled hard on the anchor rope, which had worked with the current to drag the boat farther from the shallow water.

"Start the wheels!" Captain Shreve called. But there was no time for Clark, the engineer, to get the boat moving. Suddenly there was a loud explosion and a tremendous hissing of escaping steam.

"Watch out!" someone shouted, but it was too late. Scalding steam shot over the stern deck from the end of a cylinder. Several people fell to the deck, screaming in pain. Shreve, Clark, and several others of the crew were thrown into the river by the force of the explosion. Some jumped into the Ohio in panic, for fear the whole boat was about to explode.

The people of the village at Harmar put out in small boats as quickly as they could. The sound of the explosion reached as far back as Marietta, and to Belpre, a few miles downriver. Help was soon on the way, but for some of the victims it was already too late.

Six

WHEN Shreve opened his eyes an hour or two later, he saw that he was in his bunk on the *Washington*. He felt the gentle rocking motion, but there was no sound coming from the engine. Then he remembered—the explosion, the screams—or could it have been a bad dream?

His chest hurt when he breathed. Slowly he realized that his whole body ached.

"Hello, Captain. Glad to see you coming back to this world."

The deep voice was not familiar. Gently, a hand took hold of his wrist, and he realized the stranger was a doctor.

"You are one of the lucky ones," the doctor said.

Then it was not a nightmare—the explosion had been real! He sank back into unconsciousness.

A few days later, when he had regained consciousness, he was told that seven passengers had died, mostly from breathing the scalding steam, and a deck hand had been lost in the river. Clark, along with Shreve, had been wounded but not seriously, as had four passengers.

Doctors had come from Marietta to help and within hours, the steamboat had become a floating hospital, for there was no other place to take the wounded. As for the *Washington*, little damage had been done except around the boiler area on the rear deck.

As he recovered physically, Shreve relived the accident over and over again. Could he have prevented it? What went wrong with his designs? He felt that he had caused terrible things to happen and almost wished his own life had ended. But after a few more days, he began to look ahead.

One afternoon, Clark, recovered from his injuries, came to see Captain Shreve, who was up and dressed for the first time since the accident.

"What do we do now, Captain?"

Shreve's thoughts had circled and recircled all the possibilities. He felt he had begun to think clearly and logically.

"We find out why it happened," he said to his engineer. Together, they went to the deck where the explosion had taken place. There were some shattered wooden walls, decking, railings and, of course, some damage to the cylinder that had exploded, but the rest of the steamboat was not harmed. Then they found a piece of metal from the cylinder with the safety valve still attached. It was in closed position.

"Here's our problem, Captain," Clark said. "This weight was supposed to be free to slide back, but it jammed over here. That's what kept the valve from releasing."

"That's it, all right." Shreve said. "But it worked perfectly every time we tested it. What was different this time?"

The two men thought back through the incidents before the explosion. "I think I know the answer," Shreve said. "The tests were all done with the boat freely afloat. The boat tilted when we got into the shallows alongside the island. That's the only difference in the whole thing."

He examined the mechanism carefully and then said, "I can tell you one thing. It will never happen again—not on one of my steamboats!"

"What do you mean, Captain? Do you plan to repair the *Washington* and go on?"

"Of course I do."

"After all that's happened?"

"Look, Clark. I feel terrible about the accident. You know that. But quitting now won't bring those people back to life. Nor will it help the problem of getting steamboat transportation up here where it's so badly needed." He paced the deck a full minute before he went on.

"I must repair the *Washington*. What I was working toward is still right, and my steamboat design is sound. I know it is. We'll work over the safety valve and test it in all positions. Believe me, the *Washington* will prove herself on her next voyage."

There was silence for a moment or two. Then Shreve went on. "It wouldn't be fair to my investors for me to quit now. I couldn't possibly repay them. No, I have no choice."

There was silence as the two men looked over toward the shore of the island where a clump of willows grew, their yellow-green leaves dipping into the dark water. A bluejay called harshly, breaking the summer silence.

At last Clark said, "I see your viewpoint, Captain. The whole reason for building this steamboat is still there—it's badly needed. And we both know that she's the best boat ever to float the Ohio—or the Mississippi, for that matter."

"Are you willing to stay on as my engineer? Will you work with me on this valve problem?"

Clark nodded and put out his hand. "All the way, Captain."

"Then we'll get to work. We'll float down to Louisville, keelboat style, and we'll tackle this valve design while the deck repairs are made."

"When do we start?"

"As soon as the other people on board can be moved. Check out the crew and see who'll stay with us."

The arrival at Louisville was not as Henry had planned it, but his family was relieved to see him almost fully recovered. He was glad they had made the move to Portland and could be together in this difficult time. Mary, too, had wondered if her husband would give up on his steamboat plans, but she saw the logic of his need to go on.

Many people believed the whole cause of the accident was the fact that the *Washington* had a high-pressure engine. The very sound of the words seemed to spell "danger." Shreve tried to explain what happened, until he saw that people whose minds were made up were not really interested in having them changed.

He and Clark went about the business of making mechanical repairs while carpenters replaced the damaged wooden parts. He made drawings of a new assembly for the balance arm of the safety valve and, when he was satisfied, had the parts made. First on land and then on the steamboat, level and atilt, the tests were made over and over again. The valve opened properly each time.

As he prepared the *Washington* for a fresh start, Shreve caught up with the news of other steamboats. The ill-fated *Vesuvius* had caught fire late in the summer of 1815, burning to the water line, and the cargo and most of the boat were destroyed. Even though the owners saved the machinery and rebuilt the steamboat, months passed before the *Vesuvius* could be ready for use again. In the meantime, the *Aetna* advertised for passengers and cargo for the Natchez-New Orleans trade, but people were losing confidence in steamboats. Most were used to tow sailing ships up the many miles of Mississippi River from the Gulf of Mexico to New Orleans.

In the fall of 1815, the Fulton-Livingston company had decided to show the world that the *Aetna* could do as the *Enterprise* had done and go up to Louisville. The boat traveled at a time of high water, with freight and a few passengers. The trip was very slow, as the boat had to make long stops while the crew cut wood. Then, soon after they entered the Ohio River, a wrought iron wheel shaft broke. With one paddle wheel, using poles to keep the boat headed right, they reached Henderson, Kentucky, the first town large enough to have a welder. After a two-week stopover, the repair still hadn't been made. Sixty days after leaving New Orleans, the steamboat made it to Shippingport, where the broken shaft was finally repaired.

Captain Shreve had to wait for deeper water to get his *Washington* over the Falls of the Ohio. The river began to rise in mid-September, and he advertised a departure on September 24, 1816, from Louisville to New Orleans. He had few takers for freight, and none for passenger service, but he had expected this. He knew he would have to prove that his steamboat could travel in safety before the public would have confidence in it.

"We'll go downriver on our own expense, and come back the same way if necessary," he told Clark.

When September 24 came, there were few watchers and little cheering as the *Washington* was piloted over the Falls of the Ohio and began the voyage to New Orleans. The long pointed banner—with its brave blue DON'T GIVE UP THE SHIP—streamed in the breeze, more meaningful in Shreve's

Shreve's *Ohio* was built in 1817, soon after the double-decked *Washington*, and was probably very similar in design.

mind than before. Without difficulty, the *Washington* docked in New Orleans on October 7.

Abner Duncan was the first visitor to the steamboat, coming on board soon after she was tied in place alongside the levee.

"Edward Livingston's just as stubborn as ever, Henry," he said. "He's determined to hold onto that monopoly, even though the court decisions have been in our favor. Like the last time, the jury—which Livingston tried to avoid dealing with, but I demanded—decided in favor of free navigation. Unfortunately, now Livingston has John Grymes planning their case, and Grymes is the smartest lawyer in New Orleans."

Duncan paused, and Shreve asked, "What can he do? We've got the people on our side."

"I know that, but he's looking for all possible loopholes. And he's finding them, too. He's had our last judgment set aside, and he's filed for delay after delay, postponing another hearing."

"But what do you think they'll do now that the *Washington* is here? I'm going to advertise for freight and passengers—I badly need the income."

"They'll do their best to prevent your getting out of here, Henry. Last April they forced the *Oliver Evans* to leave without cargo or passengers. Livingston ordered the captain to leave with an empty boat or he'd force him to surrender the steamboat itself."

Captain Shreve took off his cap and ran his fingers through his hair. "Yes, I heard about it," he said after a moment. "That's the boat built by Oliver Evans' son, George. It's the only other steamboat with a high-pressure engine. She made the trip safely, anyway. Maybe that will help people believe in high-pressure engines."

"Yes," Duncan said, "and that should help you get passengers and freight. Another thing on our side is that the newspapers are carrying editorials about how the monopoly is preventing free trade, saying it's bad for business."

"Well, that's good, but it doesn't seem to stop Livingston and Grymes. How are we going to handle things this time, Abner?"

"They'll send the marshal to serve papers on you—maybe even have you arrested. My advice is to let them and don't fight it. The people here remember you as a war hero and they'll really be angry if Livingston has you arrested." Duncan paused, then added, "Let them take you off to jail. Public opinion's on your side, Henry, and the people will raise a ruckus when they hear about it."

"Abner," Henry began, "I don't want to spend my time here in a prison cell—"

"You won't be there more than a few hours. Just remember, I know the law, too. Trust me."

Captain Shreve went to the customhouse to file his entry papers for the port and paid the usual fees, but he refused to pay the additional heavy costs demanded by Edward Livingston for licensing. When he returned to his steamboat, he saw that a visitor was on board. It was Edward Livingston himself. Clark had just given him a tour of the *Washington*.

Livingston was about to climb the gangplank to the levee as Shreve boarded. He waited while Shreve approached. Neither man offered his hand. Unsmiling, Livingston started up the gangplank and then turned back.

He hesitated a moment. "Shreve," he said in a gruff voice, "I'll have to admit this is a fine steamboat. You deserve well of your country, young man, but we shall be compelled to beat you if we can."

Shreve was too surprised to respond. "Good day," Livingston said and made his way up the gangplank.

Shreve advertised in the *Gazette* for freight and passengers for his return voyage, just as he said he would. Several days went by with no word from Livingston, and the time was drawing near for the departure of the *Washington*. Freight was stowed for upriver shipment, and a few passengers had purchased tickets.

Captain Shreve began to think that Livingston had given up.

"Don't count on it," Duncan told him. "Sooner or later, he'll have the marshal there looking for you."

Duncan was right. The day before the scheduled departure, the morning crowd on the levee was larger than usual, and people were crowding as close as they could to the *Washington*. It was rumored that Shreve was about to be arrested and many had come for the excitement. Sure enough, as Shreve was loading more freight the marshal, pushing his way through the crowd, called to Shreve from the levee.

Shreve strode up the gangplank.

"I have here a warrant to take possession of your steamboat, Captain," the marshal said, "plus an arrest warrant for you. You can pay ten thousand dollars bail."

"I'm not surrendering my steamboat, nor am I paying any bail," Shreve stated flatly.

The marshal was surprised. He had no choice but to arrest Captain Shreve for his defiance of the law.

Cries of disapproval came from the crowd.

"That's no way to treat Captain Shreve!" shouted a woman who was selling vegetables. "Don't you let him arrest you, Captain!"

"It's all right, folks," Shreve called out. "I'll go with the marshal, but I'll be back. Keep an eye on things here, John! There'll be more freight coming along for loading."

He marched off with the marshal, who seemed quite embarrassed. "Tell you what, Captain," he said when they'd gone down off the levee and were crossing the square. "I'll take you to Livingston's office instead of the courthouse. Let's see if you fellows can work this out peaceable-like."

As they entered Edward Livingston's law office, the clerks there looked up in surprise. One went to inform Livingston that the marshal and Shreve were there. Shreve was left waiting while the marshal was called inside. When he came out, he said, "Mr. Livingston says to tell you that you're fighting a losing battle and you'll hear from him again soon. You can go back to your steamboat, but you're not to leave New Orleans."

Shreve still had the papers the marshal had handed him in his pocket. Instead of going back to the *Washington*, he hastened to Duncan's office.

"I've got the next step ready, Captain," Duncan said. He picked up a file of papers. "We're filing a countersuit, and demanding an immediate hearing. We'll sue *them* for ten thousand dollars—for detaining your steamboat."

Duncan got fast results. A court date was set just a day ahead and a jury was quickly chosen.

"You know which way the jury will vote, Shreve," Duncan said. "Be ready to embark the following day."

It went as Duncan predicted. The two claims for ten thousand dollars canceled each other, for the jury quickly decided in Shreve's favor. But the next day, as he prepared to embark, he had another surprise. A messenger from Livingston's office came to the *Washington* and, with great politeness, asked Shreve to go with him to the law office. Mr. Livingston and Mr. Grymes wished to speak with Captain Shreve.

"What on earth for? I've got nothing to say to them."

"Please, Captain. They said it would be to your benefit."

Shreve went, mystified as to how he could benefit from a talk with his enemies. But first he sent off a note to Duncan, telling his attorney where he was going.

As Shreve entered the Livingston office, John Grymes spoke first. "Captain, why don't we get together on this matter in a sensible way? We can all make a good profit if we stop this bickering."

Shreve said, "Bickering! Is that what you call it?"

Mr. Grymes just smiled and went on smoothly. "Now here's our offer. If you advise your attorney to shape his defense so that the final verdict will support our claims, we will make you a rich man for life."

Grymes paused a moment to let this sink in. Shreve said nothing, but his thoughts were racing. It was plain to see that the big steamboat company knew they were beaten.

"We want you to work for us, the Fulton-Livingston group.

We want your ideas, the use of your steamboat *Washington*, and any other steamboats you may design. In return, we will pay you one-half of our total profits."

Shreve's head suddenly seemed to spin. He shook it so that he could think more clearly. If he took this offer, he would have the money he badly needed, for he had been without income for many months. He could come and go freely in New Orleans. He wouldn't have to worry about raising money for his next steamboat. . . .

And then he realized that the exclusive rights law would be stronger than ever. The rest of the boat builders would still be blocked, and the fight for open and free use of the rivers would be lost.

Still, how wonderful it would be to be free of this fight and of money worries. Or would it be so wonderful? What would he say to folks back home and to his fellow rivermen? Was money more important than all he'd been fighting for?

He stood up and faced the two attorneys. He knew what to say. "Thank you, gentlemen. Your offer is most generous. But my answer is no. The *Washington* and I will do fine without your help." He tipped his cap and left.

Duncan was waiting outside. Shreve reported what had taken place as the two walked rapidly back to the *Washington*. It was only one hour until sailing time.

"Get underway on time, Captain. We've got them worried now, and I can handle it from this end. Good luck!"

The *Washington* returned to Shippingport in early November. The few passengers who got off the steamboat had only good words about their voyage, which was made without the aid of flood waters to help the steam engine. Word spread that perhaps Captain Shreve's high-power, high-pressure engine might be safe after all.

Winter set in early that year and was an unusually cold season. Ice formed on the Ohio River, and one of the worst dangers to a wooden steamboat hull was to have ice pile up around it with crushing force. Captain Shreve saw that he would have to stay at home until springtime, keeping a close watch on the *Washington* until the danger had passed.

Fortunately, the spring thaw came early, and Shreve advertised that his steamboat would leave for New Orleans on March 3, 1817. It would travel non-stop, except to take on wood. He had plenty of freight and a few passengers when the day came to leave. Nine days later, the *Washington* tied up at New Orleans.

Duncan, with legal papers in hand, was waiting for him. "Livingston and Grymes are fairly fuming, Henry. They were mad as blazes last November when you turned them down, and now they've cooked up a suit that's dragged up everything you ever did against their monopoly. Look at it! It goes on and on!"

"Well, Abner, I'm not too surprised. What do they want this time?"

"They're demanding the surrender of your steamboat and ten thousand dollars to boot, because you defied the law last October and did business in Louisiana. They're going to do their best to get the *Washington* and ruin you, too."

"What's your advice, Abner?"

"As before, make them arrest you rather than offer bail. This time, insist that they take you to jail."

"While they take over the *Washington*? Not on your life!"

Duncan said, "Take it easy, Henry! I've got plans. We'll get the *Washington* on her way back—with you at the helm as usual. Don't worry. Just let me know the minute anything happens. I'll be ready."

Captain Shreve paid his usual fees except for the Fulton-Livingston license demands, as before, and unloaded his cargo. Then he announced, through an ad in the paper, that he would leave for Shippingport on March 24 with freight and passengers.

Days went by, and nothing was heard from Grymes or Livingston. Then, on Friday, March 21, rumors began to spread. The next morning a crowd gathered on the levee as before. And again the marshal came to the *Washington*, the people jeered, and he tried to avoid taking Shreve to jail.

"No, sir. I will not accept your papers. Take me to jail." Henry held out his wrists for handcuffs, and the crowd jeered even louder. The marshal refused to apply the handcuffs but took Henry's arm and they walked off together. A little group followed them, harassing the marshal all the way to the jail.

The law suit entitled "*Heirs of Fulton and Livingston* vs. *Henry M. Shreve*" was filed on March 22, and Captain Henry Shreve spent that Saturday night in jail. The next day, even though it was Sunday, Abner Duncan met with the judge. It was arranged that Captain Shreve was to be permitted to leave with the *Washington* as advertised, at five o'clock in the afternoon of Monday, March 24, without interference, upon payment of bail. Attorney Abner Duncan was to appear on his behalf at a hearing set for April 21.

The *Washington* embarked on schedule, and twenty-four days later, on April 17, with a triumphant sounding of her horn, she pulled alongside the landing at Shippingport.

Now most people realized that the *Washington* was the steamboat they had been waiting for. "This time the Mississippi has really met her master," the newspapers reported, and the words were repeated again and again.

A dinner was planned to honor Captain Shreve on the Wednesday following his return to Louisville. After many toasts, Shreve was asked to make a speech. People thought he was joking, and laughed a bit when he said that before many years steamboats would come up from New Orleans in only *ten* days.

This seemed unbelievable to people who were used to waiting months for a boat to come that far. Wasn't a twenty-four day voyage miraculous enough?

Two days before that dinner, the case of the Fulton-Livingston heirs versus Henry M. Shreve was settled in the New Orleans court, but in a strange way. The judge decided that since the Fulton-Livingston heirs were residents of New York, they could not sue Shreve, a resident of Kentucky, in a Louisiana court. This side-stepped a clear decision about the exclusive rights law, but it did help Shreve. It stopped the holders of the exclusive rights from suing those who defied it.

To Shreve's friends in New Orleans and Louisville, it was a great victory for Captain Shreve, and for free use of the rivers. In the months that followed, Livingston tried a few more times to stop other steamboats from doing business in Louisiana, but his cases failed when they came to court.

A few years later, in 1824, the Supreme Court of the United States made a decision in a case that was similar to Shreve's. The Supreme Court ruled that no state had authority over the use of any river that ran through, or was a boundary for, more than one state. This clearly made rivers such as the Ohio and the Mississippi open to all, with or without steam power, and was the foundation for all the interstate commerce laws we now have.

The Shreve case so weakened the Fulton-Livingston steamboat business in the West that in 1818, just a year after the court fight against Shreve, the company sold all its western steamboats. At the same time, Captain Shreve moved ahead rapidly in the steamboat business, building new boats to travel the rivers along with the *Washington*.

By that time, the old banner with its bold message—DON'T GIVE UP THE SHIP—had been tattered by the breezes of many voyages. The time came for Captain Shreve to fold it away carefully, a memento of a difficult battle he had fought and won—and of a time when he risked all he had for freedom on the rivers.

Seven

RIGHT after the celebration dinner in Louisville, Captain Shreve advertised for freight and passengers for his next trip to New Orleans. Long before his departure on April 30, he had signed up all he could carry. Then he reached New Orleans in record time and, quite pleased with himself, placed an ad in the *Gazette* that showed his pride. It read:

> FOR LOUISVILLE, Ken.
> The Steamboat
> *Washington*
> CAPT. SHREVE

Arrived last evening after a passage of seven days from Louisville, being 6 days underway, having touched at Henderson for cargo, where she was detained a day and night. She will be ready to receive cargo, on Wednesday 7th, and will positively sail on Thursday 15th. For freight or passage apply to Messrs. Flower and Finley, or to the captain on board. . . .

Shreve soon saw how much the opening of steamboat traffic from the upper rivers meant to the people of New

Orleans. He had known how important it was to people who lived far up the Ohio River, but now he learned that having free trade was also appreciated here. He was greeted warmly by people he had never met, as if they were old friends.

As soon as he could, he went to see Abner Duncan to learn more about the trial. He also wanted to pay him the fifteen hundred dollars he owed. The lawyer was, as usual, sitting with his feet on the desk.

As if nothing had happened in the six weeks since they had last talked, Duncan said, "Oh, hello, Shreve. Glad you stopped in."

"Glad I stopped in! Listen to you! *I'm* the one who's glad—glad I came to see you a long time ago!" Shreve was grinning. "If you hadn't said you'd take my case that first time I talked to you, I—Abner, I just don't know how I'd have made it through the whole mess."

"Whoa, Henry! You're getting carried away." Duncan smiled as he cleared a chair for his visitor. "Now sit and tell me how you're going to get rich in the steamboat business."

"First, you tell me about that day in Judge Hall's court," Shreve said.

Duncan, a satisfied look on his face, told him the details between puffs on his cigar. "Grymes and Livingston were something to behold," he said. "They seemed so sure that they would be ten thousand dollars plus one fine steamboat richer before the day was over. You should have seen their faces when the judge came through with the decision to throw the case out of court! His reason was that neither party to the suit was a resident of Louisiana." He leaned back, laughing at the memory.

"I'd have enjoyed that sight very much," Shreve said.

Then Duncan stopped laughing. "Actually," he went on, "I think Judge Hall figured his solution was the simplest way of ending this whole thing. Deep down, I believe he felt that you were right—but he had to go according to the state laws. I thought it was pretty smart of him."

"How did Livingston and Grymes take it?" Shreve asked.

"They were so mad, they could only sputter! Oh, I'm sure they'll keep trying some more, but this certainly shows the way the wind blows! You've got nothing more to worry about."

Before he left some two hours later, Shreve counted out the money he owed Duncan. "It's much easier earning money running a steamboat than doing what you had to do to earn this," he laughed. Then he became serious. "Actually, Abner, I can never pay you what I owe you. That's the truth."

No one was surprised as the *Washington* conquered the most difficult river currents. Before long, almost every boatyard along the Ohio River had a double-decked steamboat being built. Shreve had not applied for a patent on his steamboat, and it was openly copied. Though some builders stayed with the low-pressure engine and smaller boat size, the high-pressure engine was now commonly accepted as safe and more efficient.

In 1818, twelve new steamboats were registered as first-time arrivals in New Orleans, and the next year there were seventeen more. Many were modeled after Shreve's *Washington*, the successful steamboat which marked the opening of the steamboat age on the inland rivers.

When Captain Shreve had paid all his expenses, he showed a profit of seventeen thousand dollars on two voyages, all from freight charges and passenger fares. His investors each got a share, but Shreve knew his next step was to organize again and build another steamboat. He had no difficulty finding investors.

The *Ohio*, his second high-pressure steamboat, was much like the *Washington* in appearance, but quite a bit larger. Shreve built it with two engines and four boilers. This worked so well that he used more than one engine in other steamboats, including the *Napoleon*, completed soon after the *Ohio* early in 1818. Eventually, he used as many as four engines and eight boilers on a very large boat.

While his fleet grew, Captain Shreve continued at the helm of the *Washington*, taking time out for test runs on the new boats as they were completed. He was always on the watch for faults in his designs, looking for ways in which they could be improved. For example, he soon learned that intense heat caused the iron fireboxes of the *Washington* to burn out too quickly. His inventive mind went to work and, on the *Ohio* and the *Napoleon*, his redesigned fireboxes and chimney flues solved the problem.

There was plenty of business for all the new steamboats, and for keelboats, too, for the United States was growing rapidly. People flocked to the West in the years after the War of 1812. The American flag had new stars added nearly every year as more states joined the Union.

Cities were growing fast along the rivers, too. Pittsburgh, Cincinnati, Louisville, St. Louis, Natchez, Baton Rouge, and New Orleans were the principal ones. Memphis, Tennessee, organized in 1819, became a fast growing riverport on the Mississippi. After 1817, all of these cities had steamboat service and steamboats also went to the smaller towns along the tributaries of the Ohio and the Mississippi. Wherever there was a river deep enough to float a steamboat, one soon appeared.

As the West was settled, representatives in Congress heard pleas from the people of inland states and territories for improved mail service. There were still no long distance roads in the United States, and railroad building was far in the future. Early in 1819, Congress issued a call for steamboats to carry the mail. Shreve immediately ordered a new boat. It was to be small and fast, designed to carry only passengers and mail, and to be able to navigate some of the smaller rivers. Before the end of the year, the first official mail boat in the United States, Henry Shreve's *Post Boy*, was ready.

In 1821, the aging *Washington*, with Captain Shreve at the helm, went up the Missouri River with supplies for army posts at Council Bluffs in Nebraska. The Missouri was known for its many sandbars and changing channels and currents. It was

This illustration shows the Mississippi River at the mouth of the Missouri River, early in steamboat days. Snags are visible, as are a flatboat, a raft, and two steamboats.

very difficult to navigate, and its muddy waters added to the problems. Shreve had to stop to clean the *Washington*'s boilers every two or three days, for river water was used to make the steam to power the engines. It was a slow voyage, but still much faster than keelboats could travel.

At that time, the Missouri River was the only route to the northwest. It was especially important to the fur-trading companies and the United States Army. Before the *Washington*'s voyage, only one or two other high-pressure steamboats had gone to Council Bluffs, about six hundred miles from St. Louis. Fulton-type boats had tried to ascend the "Mighty

Mo," but failed. Only those steamboats that were built following Shreve's design—with high-pressure engines, and able to float in three or four feet of water—could succeed. Soon after the *Washington*'s voyage, small, high-pressure steamboats, with shallow hulls and stern paddle wheels, were being built especially for the Missouri. For more than fifty years, until a railroad was built in 1880, these steamboats provided the only transportation to the northwest.

Meanwhile, passenger service on the Mississippi and Ohio rivers was flourishing. Newspapers described these early passenger boats as "elegant," but a person traveling in them probably wasn't very comfortable. The women shared one cabin and slept in bunk beds along the sides, each curtained off from the next. They dressed in an open space in the middle and shared a washstand at one end of the cabin.

The men's cabin was larger, with bunks in tiers of three along each side. They, too, shared an open space for dressing and a crude washstand. Their open space was small, however, because a long dining table was in the center of the cabin. No man was allowed to sleep late because all had to be up and dressed before the table was set for breakfast. The women were seated when the stewards had everything ready, and then the men were allowed to sit. Serving was "family style," and he who got the bowl of a favorite food last was likely to go hungry.

Henry Shreve often piloted the *Washington* until, in 1822, the boat's wooden hull was worn out. Five or six years was old age for a steamboat because the timbers rotted. Many never reached old age due to damage from snags or explosions.

Captain Shreve's replacement for the *Washington* was to be his masterpiece. He named it the *George Washington*.

"We're going to build a steamboat such as no one ever saw before," Shreve told his boat builder in Cincinnati. "It's going to be three decks high, for starters."

He took out the detailed drawings he had been preparing ever since he'd realized he had to replace the *Washington*.

"She'll be a boat that the passengers will love," Shreve said. "We're going to have staterooms instead of open cabins. Each one will have its own bunk beds and a small space for a dressing room. Have you seen the *General Pike?*"

"Of course," the boat builder answered. "She docks here regularly. I've been all through it."

"Then you know what I'm thinking of. The *General Pike* has two groups of staterooms, besides the usual big sleeping rooms. I want to go to all staterooms—no curtained-off bunks—with just two bunks in each room. Get the idea?"

The boat builder nodded. "Sounds good, but where do people eat their meals?"

Shreve pointed out the dining space, the galleys where the meals would be prepared, and other details on his drawings.

"Now I see why you need another deck," the builder said.

"You haven't seen the half of it yet," Shreve said. He spread out another drawing. "Look here. See this broad staircase leading to the upper decks?"

"Should be beautiful, Captain."

"And picture how this grand salon will look! I want crystal chandeliers to light it and the finest of furnishings."

"I'll have to send away for the chandeliers, Captain. But those orders can be filled while we are doing the basic structure. Let's look at how you're going to make the hull strong enough to bear all that weight."

They spent hours studying the details. Shreve had designed supports for the extra weight, using heavy beams set at an angle between the first and second decks. The hull was much shallower, almost flat. All of the machinery, including four engines and eight boilers connected to two huge stacks, was placed on the main deck. The hold was to be used entirely for freight.

The upper deck of staterooms and recreation rooms took up most of the length of the boat. Each stateroom had a window from which the passengers could have a private view of the

The *George Washington*, built by Shreve in 1824, was the first of the "floating palaces" that soon became common on the Mississippi River. The artist has shortened the boat's name, but the drawing is otherwise accurate.

passing scenery. A walkway or "gallery" was built around the staterooms on the outside.

"Instead of curtains," Shreve said, "I plan to have doors leading from the public rooms into the staterooms. And to help each passenger find his own stateroom easily, I've decided to name each one for a state! That way, when a passenger comes on board, he can be told, 'You'll be staying in New York, this trip, Mr. Jones. Or would you prefer Kentucky?'"

He and the builder laughed at this idea, but it was adopted. Shreve's stateroom idea was so successful that, before long, other boat builders were also using staterooms—and naming them after states.

"There is one other very important feature that I want you to study," Shreve continued. "Each of the big paddle wheels has its own separate engines. With independent operation, the steamboat will be able to back up and turn in less space and much more efficiently."

"Hm-m-m—I don't know why no one's thought of that before now. Excellent idea, Captain Shreve. Let's get started!"

It took all of 1823 to get the *George Washington* built. In 1824, she was ready to begin the Louisville-to-New Orleans trade. She soon became a very popular boat for passengers because of the many new features. Though there was little more than scenery to entertain the women, the men had card rooms and bars and could have a lively—and expensive—voyage.

A visitor from England, Mr. W. Bullock, was a passenger on the *George Washington* in 1827. He wrote in his journal, ". . . the finest vessel I have ever seen. . . . None of the sleeping rooms have more than two beds. . . . and a gallery and verandah extends entirely around the vessel, affording ample space for exercise, sheltered from sun and rain, and commanding, from its height, a fine view of the surrounding scenery."

Before many years, the "floating palace," a steamboat modeled with only slight changes, after the *George Washington*, was common on the Mississippi. Again, Henry Shreve's inventiveness had set the pattern. Truly, he had become the "Father of the Mississippi Steamboat."

Eight

IT was 1824 and the beautiful, fast *George Washington* was plying the Mississippi and Ohio rivers. Shreve's boat was making regular voyages to New Orleans and returning to Louisville in only ten days. Seven years earlier, when Shreve had told the people of Louisville this could be expected, they had found it hard to believe. Now the prediction had come true. In fact, Captain Shreve knew the *George Washington* could make the upriver voyage in a week or less.

He knew this, but he refused to test his steamboat to set a speed record. He was unwilling to run the *George Washington* at full speed because steamboats that went too fast were very likely to be ripped open by snags. The rivers were as full of the dangerous driftwood as they had been in keelboat days.

"Three steamboats have been lost in five months, in the Mississippi, in consequence of running foul of great trunks of trees called 'sawyers,'" a newspaper reported. Many thousands of dollars were lost, as well as the lives of passengers and crew members, when the steamboats went down. And the faster the steamboats traveled, the more frequent and serious the accidents became.

To try to solve the problem, one steamboat designer built a

special, sealed-off chamber at the prow of his boat. His reasoning was that the boat wouldn't sink if it ran into a snag that ripped open the forward part of the hull. Captain Shreve didn't think this a good idea, however. It wasted cargo space, and there was no guarantee that the snag rip would come at the front.

The only cure for the problem, Shreve believed, was to clear out the planters and sawyers—get rid of them forever. But how was that to be done?

He had already begun to draw up plans for using steamboats to clear away the snags. For several years he had been hoping the United States Army Corps of Engineers might take some action to start snag clearance. He wanted to offer his ideas on how it might be done. But Congress, with its power to direct the Army Corps of Engineers, took no action. The reason was that there was no definite ruling to give the United States government responsibility for interstate rivers. Was the problem that of the states, or of the federal government?

Early in 1824, in a New York state court case, a Supreme Court decision made that point clear. Rivers that ran through more than one state, or formed interstate boundaries, were not under the control of any one state's laws. Federal government laws on interstate rivers were above those of any state.

Then, near the end of June that year, letters from the Chief Engineer's office in Washington, D. C., arrived in the mail of many steamboat captains. The circular stated that, by an act of Congress on May 24, 1824, money had been set aside to pay for the removal of "all trees which may be fixed in the bed of the river, commonly called planters, sawyers, or snags. . . ." The Army Corps of Engineers was asking for ideas about how this could be accomplished. The government realized how important good river transportation was to the growing population of the West. Added to this, the Secretary of War, in charge of the Army Corps of Engineers, was concerned about transportation of the men and supplies being sent to the new army posts west of the Mississippi.

This drawing shows the snag boat, *Capt. H. M. Shreve*, which was similar to the *Heliopolis*. Shreve is standing on top of the boilerhouse in the foreground. This is the only accurate drawing of a snag boat made during Shreve's lifetime.

Early in July, Captain Shreve mailed his drawings to Washington. He had a plan for twin steamboats attached to each other, with a man-powered windlass—a large wheel and ropes for lifting heavy objects—between the two boats. There was also equipment on the boats for sawing off the snags underwater. Shreve wrote that he was sure the snags could be removed and offered to send a model of his plan.

The next notice from Washington stated that one thousand dollars would be paid for the best idea submitted. Captain Shreve felt his ideas were worth more than a thousand dollars. If he accepted the prize, the plans would become the property of the United States government. He did not send in his model.

Soon he learned that Captain John Bruce of Kentucky had contracted with the government to begin work in the Ohio River below Louisville. Bruce had put a single paddle wheel between two steamboat hulls to move the boats. He would use hand tools to try to clear away the snags. Bruce's boat proved to be of little help, and he soon changed to flatboats. His men used hand saws, chains, and levers to try to pull up, or cut away the snags. At the end of two years they were still working in the Ohio River, not many miles from where they had started. The money Congress had set aside, supposed to clear the Ohio *and* the Mississippi, was all used up. Work was stopped.

In Washington, the original applications were checked and Shreve's drawings were found. A letter went out, offering Shreve the position of United States Superintendent of Western River Improvements. He would work as a civilian under the Army Corps of Engineers. The commission, dated December 10, 1826, was signed by President John Quincy Adams.

Captain Shreve was doing very well financially. He had a fleet of steamboats and several riverboat captains working for him, as well as the crews that operated the boats and saw to the needs of the passengers. The *George Washington* was so admired and successful that other steamboat builders were modeling their newest boats after Shreve's masterpiece. The offer from the United States government carried a salary of only six dollars a day, much less than he was making from his steamboat business.

"But what good is a steamboat business if the rivers are clogged with snags?" he asked himself. "Somebody needs to tackle this problem, and I think I can do it. If I don't do it, the rivers will continue to get worse. . . ."

Henry Shreve had never been able to resist a challenge—and this was the biggest challenge ever put before him. He accepted the job. His appointment was confirmed on January 2, 1827.

* * *

Shreve built his first snag boat, certain that it would work better than Bruce's. It had a paddle wheel on the outer side of each boat, greater engine power, and a huge windlass for pulling the snags from the water. When it was ready, he began where Bruce had left off in the Ohio River.

It took only a week or two before Shreve realized that with this boat, he couldn't make enough progress. Sawing trunks apart underwater took far too much time, and the planters—centuries-old trees that had put down roots in the river bottom—would not budge. In vain, the men strained to turn the windlass, with its heavy chains and hooks attached to the planter. Even with the steam engines running, backing the twin boats to add to the pulling power, the huge, old snags remained firmly in place.

After talking it over with his crew, Shreve said, "We really don't have to pull them up. All we have to do is break them off far enough down that a steamboat can ride above them safely. That will do it."

"But how can you break them off down under the water?" one of his foremen asked.

"I'm going to work on it. I have an idea for a way to use the full force of the steam engines. I think it will do the job."

Once again, he worked night after night at his desk. He came up with a design for a snag boat that would break the tree trunks near the river bottom, using the full power of the steam engines. The windlass would also be steam-powered and have a sixty-five-foot chain, with a noose at the end, to pull out the snags.

This snag boat had plenty of engine power to do more than move the twin hulls. The steam power would handle most of the work. This included pulling the logs onto a saw table where they were cut and then pushed back into the river.

The part of the plan that he felt was most important, however, was his way of breaking off the snags. Near the front of the twin hulls there would be a huge, wedge-shaped, iron-covered, wooden connecting beam. This wedge was pointed forward and tilted downward. With full steam power, the snag boat could hit a planter so forcefully that the ancient tree trunk would snap off near the river bottom. The windlass would haul it out of the river, and it would be sawed up and taken away.

"It won't work!" a few other captains said when they saw Shreve's plans. "The steamboats will just back off, and the jar will bring on an explosion. A waste of money to even try it!"

Captain Shreve, however, was convinced his ideas were sound. He urged the Chief Engineer to get Congress to give him the money to build his snag boat. He had spent many an hour studying his drawings to make sure the steamboats themselves would not be damaged. He wrote later that this had been very difficult. He had worked on his plans until he felt his design was right and "the concussion between the snag and the snag-beam would not dislocate the boilers on the boat."

Approval didn't come quickly. Another steamboat captain was so against letting Shreve build the boat that he wrote to the Secretary of War. He said that building it would be "a useless expenditure of time and money."

Then a group of steamboatmen, who knew Shreve, sent a petition to the secretary, requesting that Shreve be allowed to test his idea. Though the secretary couldn't understand how the invention could work, he knew the snags had to be removed. Hoping he wasn't making a terrible mistake, he approved the building of a trial snag boat.

The actual work of building the first snag boat was done at the boatyard in New Albany, Indiana. Each of the twin steamboats was one hundred twenty-five feet long and twenty-five feet wide, with a ten-foot space between the two boats. Into that space the steam-powered windlass was set. The wedge-shaped beam between the two hulls was covered with iron plate one-fourth of an inch thick. It was finished on July 22, 1829, and named the *Heliopolis*.

To test the *Heliopolis*, Shreve demonstrated its power by attacking a sawyer with a trunk three-and-one-half feet in diameter and rooted twenty feet deep in the Ohio River. The great chain was lowered, fitted over the trunk, and pulled snug. The paddle wheels turned and the heavy beam struck hard against the ancient tree. There was a thud and a cracking sound as the tree snapped loose. Shreve's plan worked! The wheels groaned and the chains clanked as the trunk was hauled up and out "with the greatest of ease," as Shreve himself wrote.

Five weeks from the day the *Heliopolis* was tested, the work in the Ohio was finished and the snag boat moved into the Mississippi River. A few months later, a newspaper reporter wrote that Shreve had made a three hundred-mile stretch of the Mississippi as "harmless as a mill pond."

In 1831, a second snag boat, the *Archimedes*, was completed so that the clearing could be done faster. With two crews working, progress was rapid, and the Arkansas River was added to the project.

All seemed to be going well for Henry Shreve. In 1828, his old friend Andrew Jackson had been elected President of the United States, and he was re-elected in 1832. Jackson renewed Shreve's contract at a higher salary, giving him three thousand dollars a year instead of six dollars per working day. Life was going smoothly—almost too smoothly—and Henry Shreve was ready for a new challenge.

It came very soon, in a letter from the Chief Engineer dated September 5, 1832. As he read it, Captain Shreve's mind went back to early in 1815 when he had gone up the Red River, in Louisiana, on the *Enterprise*. Again he saw that huge blockage of driftwood, the Great Raft.

For years, the people of Louisiana had been sending petitions to Congress, asking that something be done to open the Red River. At first, the Red River did not seem very important to officials in Washington. But now, with Americans in Texas, Indian problems in the West, and Fort Towson far up the Red River, the time had come for attention to the problem. The Red River was the only practical route to Texas and the southwestern army posts.

The army had sent a lieutenant with a company of men to Louisiana to check the situation.

"The Raft is impossible to remove," was the lieutenant's report. He recommended that canals be dug for steamboats to bypass the huge mass of driftwood. The canals would cover between one hundred fifty and two hundred miles. While they would be very expensive to dig and would need work constantly, this seemed to be the only possibility.

This report went to the Chief Engineer, Colonel Charles Gratiot. Gratiot didn't like the idea of digging all those canals that would be constantly filling up with silt. In his letter to Shreve, the Chief Engineer raised the question that challenged the Captain. Would it be possible to remove the Raft? Could steamboats be taken down there, start at the foot of the Raft, and pull it apart?

Shreve wrote back on September 29. Yes, he believed the Raft could be removed. Canal building was not the way to solve this problem and, in Shreve's opinion, would be more expensive than removing the great mass of driftwood. In addition, clearing it away would have another advantage. It would drain the many acres of land that had become bayous and swamps because of the blocked river channel. Even though others said it was impossible, Shreve was sure it could be done.

Ordinary steamboats could not do the job, however. Shreve would need to take the *Archimedes* down to the Red River, plus two or three worker steamboats, other boats, and tools. With the *Archimedes*, he could force chunks of the driftwood mass to break loose. Yes, he could do the job.

Colonel Gratiot agreed. Not much money was available— only a little over twenty thousand dollars—but once Shreve had proved the Raft could be removed, Gratiot would ask for more. Yes, the *Archimedes* could be taken down there, plus the one hundred and fifty-nine men Shreve had requested and whatever else he thought necessary.

During the winter months, Captain Shreve made arrangements for the other projects on which he was working to continue, using the *Heliopolis*. He would personally take on this greatest challenge of his career—the attack on the Great Raft.

Nine

NATCHEZ, Mississippi, lay shrouded in predawn mist on April 3, 1833. The mists curtained a fleet of boats lined up along the riverfront, assembled there preparing for the remainder of the trip to the Great Raft of the Red River. Three small worker steamboats, and several keelboats and rafts were at anchor, waiting for the time to leave. With her great, eighteen-foot windlass wheels rising above the mists, the *Archimedes* stood among them like a mother duck, her ducklings clustered about.

Captain Shreve, on board the steamboat *Java*, was already up and at work. He had much to do and many details to check on that day. Natchez was the final stop before the fleet entered the Red River. Last minute purchases must be made there, for there were only small settlements ahead.

Departure time was planned for late afternoon. Shreve spent the day making final arrangements with his crew and going over the equipment. As the afternoon wore on, he completed his rounds and wrote a report to Gratiot, saying he expected to arrive at the Great Raft on April 9. Natchez was the last town on the Mississippi with regular mail service and, as darkness closed in, Shreve sent his report to the post office.

Then he blew three long blasts from the *Java*'s steam horn, signaling that all should be ready to leave. As steam pressure came up, he boarded the *Archimedes* and took over the wheel. The small steamboats—the *Java*, *Pearl*, and *Souvenir*—puffed along behind the snag boat as the fleet eased out into the Mississippi. Through the night they moved downstream toward the mouth of the Red River, about sixty miles to the south.

When they reached the Red, the steamboats waited for the keelboats and flatboats, then took them in tow. Slowly the procession made its way upstream. Along the way, Captain Shreve concentrated on finding the safest channel. He also made notes on what needed to be done to improve this lower part of the river.

There were many jutting trees and shallow sandbars where driftwood might catch if it were floating down the river. Shreve's plan for getting rid of the wood from the Great Raft was to set it afloat. He hoped it would drift all the way to the Mississippi, and then on to the Gulf of Mexico. That was the method commonly used to dispose of the logs cut from snags, but as he went up the Red, he became quite concerned. New rafts could form behind him all too easily. Perhaps there was a better way. . . .

When they reached Alexandria, a small village on the south bank of the Red, Shreve noted another situation that would need special attention. There was a rock shelf, or reef, across the river bed, and some rough, shallow water. Fortunately, the Red was in its high-water stage. With care, the *Archimedes* could get over the natural dam the rocks formed. But what about the river's low-water stage? He made notes and sketches as the fleet continued on its way upstream.

About seven hundred winding miles of the rust-colored river had to be navigated to reach the foot of the Great Raft. They were almost there when they reached the little settlement of Natchitoches late on April 10, already a full day behind Shreve's goal to reach the Raft. To Shreve's surprise, the town was no longer on the river. The floods of 1832 had

This oil painting, completed by Lloyd Hawthorne in 1970, is titled "Captain Henry M. Shreve Clearing the Great Raft from Red River, 1833–38." The snag boat shown is the *Archimedes*.

shifted the river's course, and now Natchitoches lay five miles west of the Red. The people of this settlement had hoped their town would become a great river port once the Raft was removed, but the river had spoiled their plans. Nevertheless, a number of settlers wished Captain Shreve and his men well in their gigantic task.

Early the next morning, the fleet moved on and soon was approaching the foot of the driftwood mass. The flatboats and keelboats were released from tow and the crews prepared for work. Captain Shreve could scarcely wait to test his snag boat against the Raft to see if his plans would work.

"Get up full steam power," he ordered the engineer on the *Archimedes*. The men were seeing the huge mass for the first time. They looked it over while the *Archimedes*'s pressure was building. Captain Shreve lined up the equipment and gave orders for tackling the job.

The Great Raft appeared to be an unending island that almost filled the river channel. A growth of vines, willows, and cottonwood trees covered it. Actually, the Raft was made up of thousands of logs and trees that had piled up there for centuries. Year after year at floodtime, whole trees had been torn loose from the riverbanks, often many miles up the Red. Where the river slowed or grew shallow, they stacked up, bound together by new root and vine growth. Over the years, aged logs rotted and soil formed on top, where new growth sprouted. In the oldest sections, roots reached down to the river bottom, attaching what had once been a floating island firmly in place. The tangled mass now looked as if it would be impossible to tear apart.

It also was difficult for Shreve to decide which watery path around the Raft was the channel of the Red, and which was just a swampy side pool, or bayou. There was little current, and Shreve's practiced eye couldn't detect it. The Great Raft so blocked the Red that the river simply spread out over the land. A small boat trying to make its way upstream might choose the wrong way and find itself in a shallow lake without an outlet. It would have to go back and try another waterway.

Looking about, Captain Shreve found the solution to the problem of getting rid of the loosened sections of the Raft. With such a sluggish current, setting the logs adrift would definitely not work. As they approached the blockade, however, Shreve had noticed the swampy bayous. Why not push the driftwood into first one and then another? This would serve two purposes: it would get rid of the wood, and at the same time fill up the bayous, forcing the water to flow back into the Red. This was the plan he would follow.

By ten o'clock, Captain Shreve had the *Archimedes* moved into position and ready to take its first bite out of the awesome tangle of driftwood. The captain was on board the snag boat, showing where it was to strike with its heavy, iron-clad beam. The crash came. The windlasses creaked and chains clanked.

The crew, stripped to the waist in the heat of a southern spring day, was armed with poles with spiked ends. Men leaped to places where the logs were parting, ready to push with all their strength. The machinery groaned, steam hissed, and the crew shouted above the din. The first chunk of the ancient Raft broke away.

When the loud cheers quieted, the three smaller steamboats gathered around the *Archimedes* like worker bees around their queen. They shoved and prodded the loosened clumps of logs, herding them to the mouth of the bayou Captain Shreve had chosen as the first to be filled. They rammed them in, chunk after chunk.

At the end of the first day's work, the Great Raft was five miles shorter. Captain Shreve was jubilant. The Raft could definitely be removed! On May 8, in his report to General Gratiot, Shreve wrote that they had progressed about forty miles.

Section after section of the blockade was torn away. As clumps were stuffed into first one bayou and then another, the water returned to the river channel where it belonged. The sluggish water below the foot of the Raft was transformed to a gently flowing river. Then progress slowed. The raft became more solid, more resistant as the looser foot was pulled away and the massive center approached.

The work went on day after day, and the warm spring became a sizzling summer. The men fought mosquitoes and snakes, working in the suffocating, damp air until they were dripping wet. Sometimes they came upon a family of alligators, looking very much like the ancient driftwood until one was struck with the steel point of a prod. Heavy boots were worn at all times.

In June, the men were finding this situation unlike any they had worked in before. The humidity was close to one hundred percent, and temperatures continued to climb. Illness began to spread among the work force.

The foreman came to Captain Shreve, much disturbed. "The men are threatening to quit if we go much farther,

Captain. They just can't take this heat. They're really afraid they'll take the fever and die."

"Yes," Shreve agreed, "we'll have to call off work for the summer months. I'd like to go on just a little farther. There's a trading post three miles ahead, and I want to make it our stopping place. It's called Bennett and Cane's, at Coate's Bluff. I promise we'll stop there, and we can store some of our equipment at the settlement."

With this goal in mind, the foreman was able to urge the men on for a little longer. On June 23, they reached Coate's Bluff. They could see an Indian village of the Caddo tribe, a government agent's cabin, and just upriver, Bennett and Cane's trading post. This was the place that would become the city of Shreveport, Louisiana, in a few years.

Behind them, Shreve's crew had opened the way for steamboat passage for seventy miles. The men were surprised to learn that land developers were arriving along the river, almost in the wake of the workboats. They were buying tracts of government-owned land that, once worthless, could now be sold as farmland. The drained soil was rich and loose, ideal for growing cotton. The drier lands away from the river could be sold, too, for now steamboats could take farm produce to markets.

Captain Shreve left the flatboats and some of the equipment behind when the crew boarded the other boats for the return trip to Ohio. The work would go on when the summer ended. Back in his Louisville office, Shreve wrote a long report to General Gratiot. He urged the Chief Engineer to get Congress to appropriate more funds as quickly as possible, and reported that the winter months would be the best working season. He'd like to return in November.

But Congress did not act fast enough for the crew to head back when cooler weather came in 1833. Captain Shreve spent that winter and the following spring and summer working on other projects. He hated not returning to the Red River Raft. He was annoyed at Congress' slowness to approve funds to go on, for he knew it would cost more in the long run. Driftwood would continue to accumulate, adding more to the labor of completing the task.

Finally, in the summer of 1834, Congress approved the money Shreve needed for another season of work. Shreve set the date for departure and advertised for a larger crew than he'd had before. The men would go down in November and work through the winter months, quitting before summer heat. Three hundred men were hired, and they started down the Ohio on November 14.

The water level was low. When the fleet reached Alexandria, there was so little water flowing over the reefs that steam power couldn't be used. The three worker steamboats were warped through this passage with great care. Everything that could possibly be removed from them was taken off and carried upstream to a place where the water deepened. The *Archimedes* went last, eased carefully over the ledge after much needed rain raised the water level a few inches. Shreve had recommended to Gratiot that the reef be broken up and removed, but approval for funding was even slower in coming than the monies for the Raft work.

On December 10, the crew reached the place where the Raft break-up had begun two years earlier. With the water at low level, Shreve could see the need for removing even more tree growth along the riverbanks, and snags that lay open to view. Slowly, they worked their way up the river to Coate's Bluff.

There many changes were already taking place. Small steamboats now puffed their way to a landing, and new buildings had been added to the settlement. The Caddo Indians had decided to sell their land back to the government and move farther west. Buyers were eager to invest in those lands, too. Bennett and Cane's trading post was doing a good business.

There was great cheering from a small crowd on the banks as the *Archimedes* bit into the Great Raft once again on January 20, 1835. The tough, resisting heart of the Raft made progress slow. In this area, the river was so spread out with lakes and bayous and so winding that it was hard for Shreve to tell where the original channel had been. A canal was dug across a neck of land to straighten the river and get a better flow of water. This created a good channel, and then another loop of the river was closed off with wood from the Raft, improving the situation even more. These projects, and the toughness of the Raft, made progress slow. Only a few miles of the Great Raft had been removed when the working season ended in mid-April. The men agreed to return the next season, to start in the fall, and leave in the early spring before the intense heat and humidity came.

Congress acted more quickly in 1835, and in the fall the crew was back at work, tearing at the Great Raft above Coate's Bluff until early summer. The Texas Revolution, with many Americans involved, had begun. The famous battle at the Alamo, in which Davy Crockett, Jim Bowie, and other Americans lost their lives, was on March 6, 1836. Victory for the Americans took place on April 21. The possibility that Texas would become a state made it even more important to get the Red River opened.

That same winter and spring, more people came to Coate's Bluff. They saw money-making opportunities as the river was opened. A group of them formed a company to organize a town, selling shares to people who wanted to invest their money. It would be named Shreve's Town, after the man whose work had opened the river. Captain Shreve was invited to become a partner in this company and to draw up a plan for the center of the town. He did so, naming several of the streets after heroes of the Texas Revolution. Shreve's Town was soon renamed Shreveport, because it had indeed become a port. Steamboats came all the way up from New Orleans. In a few years, Shreveport became a large, important city in Louisiana, second in size only to New Orleans.

Captain Shreve had hoped to clear away the last of the Great Raft before the work season ended. That was not to be—nine miles were left. Back they came in the autumn, this time with the *Eradicator*, a new snag boat. The aging

Archimedes had retired after tackling a snag too large for its rotting planks. The *Eradicator* cleared all but a quarter of a mile of the once huge barricade when the season ended in 1837. This seemed such a short distance, but the men, fighting illness and slapping at mosquitoes, could work no longer. Shreve was frustrated to think that steamboats still could not go all the way to Fort Towson.

Far from the scene of Red River Raft, with little idea of the problems faced by Captain Shreve, Congress argued again about funding for the project. They seemed to overlook the fact that it was already paying its way in sales of government land and in crops harvested where there had once been swamps. Funding was delayed, and it was not until 1839 that the last segment of the Great Raft was broken up. As Captain Shreve finished his clean-up of new driftwood, he warned the Army Corps of Engineers that a new raft would form unless preventive work was done each year. For Shreve, however, the tremendous task was completed.

The Red River was opened, and its rusty waters, now with an easy-to-follow channel, flowed with a current of two to three miles per hour. Flooded land was drained and crops were planted. At Shreveport, cotton was loaded onto steamboats and shipped downriver to market. Often, the riverfront bustled with a long line of steamboats loading and unloading their shipments. Once almost a wilderness, these lands were now productive. Accepting the challenge of an "impossible" task, Captain Shreve had proved that it could be done.

Author's Note

THREE years after he had completed the Red River project, in September of 1841, Captain Shreve received a letter notifying him that he was no longer Superintendent of Western River Improvements. This situation came about when a different political party came into power—not the party for which Shreve had always voted. William Henry Harrison was inaugurated on March 20, 1841, but his term as President ended in two weeks. After the inauguration he came down with pneumonia and, on April 4, he died. Vice-president John Tyler became president, and many of his political friends asked to be appointed to government positions.

In the letter, Shreve was praised for the work he had done. He was told to turn over all the equipment to another man. This included a fleet of five snag boats, the last of which was named the *Henry M. Shreve*.

Captain Shreve felt it was too late to begin again as a steamboat builder and owner. He was almost fifty-six years old, but was still well and strong, not ready to retire. Fortunately, he had made a very good decision back in the summer of 1836.

In that year, after he had returned from the Red River, he

was asked to go to St. Louis. The people of that city wanted him to see what could be done to keep the Mississippi River from changing its course to the east, threatening to leave the city without a riverfront.

While he was working on this problem, he saw an advertisement in the newspaper that interested him. Old pasture lands were for sale, located northwest of the city. They were left over from the days when St. Louis was a French village. Henry and Mary Shreve decided to bid on three hundred acres of this long unused land.

This pleased Mary, for St. Louis had come to mean much to her. She had joined her husband on his trip in 1836 because she wanted to visit their daughter Rebecca, who was now married and lived there. The Shreves' three-year-old granddaughter, Harriet, was with Mary. Shreve's older daughter, Harriet, had died soon after the birth of her baby, and her husband, John Reel, placed the baby in Mary's care. In St. Louis, there was another grandchild, Henry Shreve Carter, about the same age as little Harriet, and also a second Carter baby.

The Shreves bought the land and made arrangements for the building of a large home before they went back to Louisville. The new house was ready in 1838, and they had moved from Louisville to St. Louis County.

When he lost his job as Superintendent of Western River Improvements, Henry Shreve decided to become a farmer. As always, he put all his energy into developing the land to make it productive. Gallatin Place, as the Shreves named their new home, became a thriving farm. There were barns, shops, stables, plus houses for the people Shreve hired to work for him. In those days, all the work of a farm was hand labor, and it took about twenty people to care for a three-hundred-acre farm and a large house.

But the river was still in Henry's blood. He bought a warehouse near the busy landing in St. Louis and made excuses to spend time along the riverfront. He must have felt great satisfaction as he saw long lines of steamboats nose into

In the 1840s, St. Louis, Missouri, was a busy city. Steamboats crowded the riverfront as they prepared to carry passengers and goods on the inland rivers of America.

the docks. All followed the basic plan of the double-decked, double-stacked *Washington* of 1815, with added improvements. Many were luxury passenger packets, not very different from his *George Washington*.

Shreve's son-in-law, Walker Carter, went into the steamboat business, too, and often his friends came up to Gallatin Place to get to know "Mr. Steamboat" himself. Older riverboat captains, who had known Shreve for many years, also came to talk over the days gone by.

There were always grandchildren around, and the big house was seldom quiet. Harriet Reel continued to live with her grandparents, and the Carter children loved to visit Gallatin Place. Children of the Blair family came to visit, too, especially at Christmas. Grandpa Shreve would saddle Rock, the aging horse given to him by President Jackson, and bring him out for the small children to ride. Young and old would gather around the big dining table for the holiday feasts that his wife planned.

When Christmas came in 1844, Mary Shreve became ill. She died early in 1845. Henry walked about the farm restlessly, hating to spend time in the house that seemed so empty. A housekeeper, Lydia Rodgers, was hired to come live at Gallatin Place. Miss Rodgers was educated, intelligent, and Shreve spent his evenings talking with her. Before she had been there a year, the two were married. Shreve seemed to grow younger, especially after a baby girl, Mary, was born in 1847. A second baby girl, Florence, arrived in 1849.

Captain Shreve was respected. He was often referred to as the person who had done the most to help St. Louis become a thriving city. When telegraph lines reached there in December, 1847, he was the person selected to send the first "wire"—a message to President Polk in Washington, D. C. Shreve also kept a hand in business. When the Mexican War ended in victory, the idea that a railroad should begin at St. Louis and run west to the Pacific coast developed. Shreve, unlike some other older steamboatmen, felt that the railroad and steamboat were both needed. He was one of the men who formed the Pacific Railroad Company early in 1849.

Then, in late spring of 1849, an epidemic of cholera swept through St. Louis. One of the Carter children died. On that day, a fire broke out on a steamboat tied at the riverfront. A strong wind fanned the flames, and they spread. Whipped along by the wind and fed by dry timbers, flames spread over a half-mile of docked steamboats within thirty minutes. Twenty-three boats burned to the water line.

The fire swept up the sloping riverfront, where bales and barrels were stacked on the cobblestone pavement. From there the fire spread to nearby warehouses and into the business district. Shreve's warehouse burned in only a few hours.

This seemed too much for the old captain. His health

began to fail, and he dropped out of his civic activities, including the railroad company. Cholera took the lives of two more of his grandchildren and then, the crowning blow, his baby daughter, Florie. For the first time in his life, Henry Miller Shreve gave up the fight. His work was done. He died on March 6, 1851, aged sixty-five. In a cemetery on a bluff above the Mississippi, he was laid to rest, his monument facing the river.

    The rivers that once beckoned to Henry Miller Shreve are still part of the ongoing story of American people striving for a better life. Though one seldom hears a steamboat whistle—the sound Henry Shreve once called the "sweetest music in the world"—huge barges, carrying bulky cargo and pushed by diesel-powered workboats, still travel on the river. These have replaced the stately steamboats, with their paddle wheels churning the water. The barges seem much less glamorous in today's world of sleek, rapid transportation on land, in the air, and even in space. Still, they serve the needs of the people, as Shreve's *Washington* did in its day.

    The steamboat represents a slower-paced time that some people look back to with nostalgia. There are a few pleasure steamboats still plying the rivers. Should you someday see one of them—or possibly even ride on one—try to imagine what would have happened if there had not been an energetic man with an inventive mind, a man who could keep on when the going was rough, and who held to his beliefs. Without Henry Miller Shreve, our history would have been quite different.

Henry Miller Shreve
1785–1851
A Chronology

October 21, 1785	Henry Miller Shreve is born, Burlington County, New Jersey.
August, 1788	Shreve's family moves to George Washington farms, Fayette County, southwestern Pennsylvania.
Spring, 1800	Shreve begins career as riverboatman.
December, 1803	United States completes Louisiana Purchase.
1804–1806	Lewis and Clark travel the Missouri River to explore the Northwest.
Spring, 1807	Shreve, age 21, becomes owner of keelboat; makes first fur-trading voyage to St. Louis, Missouri.
August 17, 1807	Robert Fulton's *Clermont* is successfully tested in the Hudson River, New York.
Winter, 1811	Shreve builds keelboat for New Orleans trade; marries Mary Blair; builds home in Brownsville, Pennsylvania.

April, 1811	Robert Livingston, partner of Robert Fulton, acquires exclusive rights to use of steamboats in Louisiana; Fulton-Livingston partnership begins construction of steamboat for use on Ohio and Mississippi rivers.
November 28, 1811	Shreve's first child, Harriet Louise, is born.
January, 1812	First Fulton steamboat arrives in New Orleans.
June 18, 1812	War of 1812 begins.
October 3, 1813	Shreve's second child, Rebecca Ann, is born.
December, 1813	Shreve becomes part owner of steamboat, the *Enterprise*.
December 1, 1814	Shreve leaves Pittsburgh, Pennsylvania, with load of munitions on the *Enterprise* to help defend New Orleans.
December 15, 1814	*Enterprise* and crew taken for military service by General Andrew Jackson in New Orleans.
December 24, 1814	War of 1812 officially ended.
January 3–4, 1815	On the *Enterprise*, Shreve successfully runs British blockade to Fort St. Philip.
January 8, 1815	Battle of New Orleans; Shreve mans gun on defense line.
January 19, 1815	News received by General Jackson of official end of War of 1812.
April 8, 1815	Shreve's only son, Hampden Zane, is born.

June 26, 1815	*Enterprise* returns to Brownsville, Pennsylvania; first steamboat to travel up Mississippi and Ohio rivers.
Fall, 1815	Shreve begins building the *Washington*, first double-decked steamboat.
Spring, 1816	Death of Hampden Zane Shreve; family moves to Louisville, Kentucky.
June 3–7, 1816	*Washington*'s maiden voyage from Wheeling, Virginia, ends in explosion near Marietta, Ohio.
March–April, 1817	*Washington*, repaired and back in service, is hailed as first practical steamboat for western rivers.
April 21, 1817	Successful end of legal battle against Fulton-Livingston partnership. Free use of Louisiana waters by non-Fulton steamboats is granted.
Summer, 1817	Shreve builds steamboats *Ohio* and *Napoleon*.
Fall, 1819	*Post Boy*, first U.S. mail steamboat, built by Shreve.
1823–1824	*Washington* goes out of service; Shreve builds the *George Washington*, first of the "floating palace" steamboats.
December 10, 1826	Shreve becomes United States Superintendent of Western River Improvements.
July 22, 1829	Completion of Shreve's *Heliopolis*, first successful snag boat.
April 3, 1833	Shreve begins breaking up the Great Raft of the Red River.

Summer, 1836	Founding of Shreveport, Louisiana. Shreve buys land in St. Louis County, Missouri.
Summer, 1838	Shreve family moves near St. Louis, Missouri.
February 15, 1839	Removal of Great Raft is completed; Red River opened to steamboat traffic.
September 11, 1841	Shreve's appointment as Superintendent of Western River Improvements ends.
February 25, 1845	Death of Mary Blair Shreve.
1846–1849	Shreve marries Lydia Rodgers. Two daughters, Mary and Florence, are born.
May 17, 1849	Fire sweeps St. Louis riverfront, destroys Shreve warehouse and business section. One of Shreve's grandchildren dies from cholera. Shreve's health begins to fail.
January, 1851	Shreve's infant daughter, Florence, dies from cholera.
March 6, 1851	Death of Henry Miller Shreve.

The people of Shreveport, Louisiana, honor Captain Henry Miller Shreve with this statue, placed at the riverfront in 1967.

Living History

To bring the story of Henry Miller Shreve—and river history—more alive, there are wonderful places for you to visit.

One is the Ohio River Museum at Marietta, Ohio. There you can go aboard the old towboat, the *W. P. Snyder*, and see the quarters in which the crew lived, the great paddle wheel, and the steam engine that turned it. On the grounds are a full-sized flatboat and a pilot house that came from an old steamboat. Inside the museum are pictures of some of Henry Miller Shreve's boats and models of many steamboats. For more information, you can write to the Ohio River Museum, 601 Front Street, Marietta, Ohio 45750.

If you are in the area, spend a whole day on Mud Island, at the riverfront in Memphis, Tennessee. You can follow a five-block-long replica of the Mississippi River, from the mouth of the Ohio River to the Gulf of Mexico. This river model is narrow enough for you to step across at some places; at others, you have to use bridges. Inside the museum, you will see models and drawings of steamboats and snag boats and can read about Captain Shreve's work. On the deck of a steamboat, you can walk through life-size rooms and see real high-pressure steamboat engines. For more information, write to Mud Island, 100 N. Main, Suite 2810, Memphis, TN 38103.

In the Louisville, Kentucky, area, new locks have replaced those that allowed steamboats to avoid the Falls of the Ohio in the Louisville and Portland Canal of 1830. Across the river, at Clarksville, Indiana, one can still see the old Falls, though there is little flow of water over them. Nearby is the Howard Steamboat Museum, at Jeffersonville, Indiana, in the mansion built by the owner of the Howard Shipyards. Steamboats were built in these shipyards from 1834 on. In the museum are relics from old steamboats, as well as many steamboat models.

Steamboat models are often on display in museums and libraries in many of the river cities, such as St. Louis, Missouri, and Cincinnati, Ohio. Another excellent place to learn about steamboat history is in the Museum of History and Technology at the Smithsonian Institution in Washington, D. C.

You can also ride on an excursion boat modeled after old steamboats. There are some, such as the *Delta Queen*, that have staterooms for long voyages between cities. There are also many that take short river trips lasting an hour or two.

Whether you are looking at a steamboat model in a museum, or climbing aboard an excursion boat modeled after the real thing, you can imagine the days when the rivers were young and Captain Shreve was at the helm.

Photo Credits

Page ii: Courtesy National Portrait Gallery, Smithsonian Institution, Washington, D.C.

Page 11: Reprinted from *The Life of Robert Fulton* by Thomas W. Knox, New York, 1890.

Page 21: Reprinted from *Up the Heights of Fame and Fortune and Routes Taken by the Climbers to Become Men of Mark* by Frederick Brent Read, Cincinnati, 1873.

Page 39: Reprinted from *The Western Pilot: Containing Charts of the Ohio River and the Mississippi . . .* by Samuel Cumings, Cincinnati, 1837.

Page 62: Courtesy of The Mariners' Museum, Newport News, Virginia; reproduced from an old woodcut.

Page 75: Courtesy of The St. Louis Mercantile Library Association; reproduced from *Das Illustrirte Mississippithal*, Germany, 1854.

Page 78: Courtesy of Captain Frederick Way, Jr.; reproduced from an old woodcut.

Page 83: Reproduced from a lithograph by August A. Von-Schmidt, St. Louis, 1847.

Page 92: Copyright © 1970, the R. W. Norton Gallery, Shreveport, Louisiana. Used by permission.

Page 101: Courtesy of The St. Louis Mercantile Library Association; reproduced from *Route from Liverpool to the Great Salt Lake Valley* by Frederick Percy, Liverpool, 1855.

Page 108: Courtesy of *The Shreveport Times*.

Index

Adams, John Quincy, 84
Aetna (steamboat), 12, 34, 37, 40, 41, 61
Alamo, 97
Alexandria (village), 91, 96
Allegheny River, 2, 13
Archimedes (snag boat), 87, 88, 90, 91, 92–94, 96–97, 98
Arkansas River, 87

Battle of Lake Erie, 54
Battle of New Orleans, 29–30
Boat builders, 2, 45, 67, 73, 79, 84
Bowie, Jim, 97
Brownsville, 3, 4, 6, 8, 9, 45
Bruce, Capt. John, 84, 85
Bullock, W., 79

Caddo Indians, 95, 96
Carter, Henry Shreve, 100
Carter, Walker, 101
Clark (engineer), 56, 58, 59–60, 61, 64
Clark, Robert, 43–44, 48–49
Clermont (steamboat), 4
Coate's Bluff, 95, 96, 97
Council Bluffs, Neb., 74–75
Crockett, Davy, 97

Delta Queen (steamboat), 110
Dispatch (steamboat), 43, 51, 52

Duncan, Abner, 31–36, 38, 51, 63–69, 72–73

Enterprise (steamboat), 8, 9–15, 16, 18–31, 33, 35–36, 37–41, 44, 52
Eradicator (snag boat), 97–98
Evans, George, 63
Evans, Oliver, 42, 46, 63

Falls of the Ohio, 14, 38–40, 50, 52, 62, 110
Flatboats, 2, 3, 84, 91, 92, 95
Fort St. Denis, 30
Fort St. Philip, 19–20, 24, 25–26, 29, 41
Fort Towson, 87, 98
French, Daniel, 8, 9, 10, 41–43, 44, 49, 52
Fulton, Robert, 1, 4, 5, 11, 33
Fulton boats, 4–5, 14, 43, 44, 45
Fulton-Livingston Company, 32, 61; monopoly, 5, 6, 13, 18, 31–36, 37–38, 51–52, 63–70, 72–73

General Pike (boat), 77
George Washington (steamboat), 76–80, 81, 84, 101
Gillespie, Neal, 43–44, 48–49
Gratiot, Col. Charles, 88, 90, 94, 96

113

Great Raft of the Red River, 30, 88–89, 90–98, 99
Gregg, Israel, 51, 52
Grymes, John, 63, 64, 66–67, 68, 72–73
Gulf of Mexico, 8, 20, 61, 91

Hall, Judge, 72
Harrison, William Henry, 99
Heliopolis (snag boat), 86–87, 89
Henry M. Shreve (snag boat), 99
Howard Steamboat Museum, 110

Jackson, Andrew, 8–9, 16–18, 19–24, 27, 28–31, 47, 52, 87, 102
Java (steamboat), 90, 91

Keelboats, 3, 4, 6, 14–15, 17, 18, 19, 30, 74, 91, 92

Lane, Noah, 45–47, 55
Lawrence (ship), 54
Lawrence, James, 54
Livingston, Edward, 33–34, 35, 51, 63, 64, 65, 66, 68, 70, 72–73
Livingston, Robert, R., 4, 5, 33, 34
Louisiana: law restricting free river trade, 1, 5, 18, 31, 32, 33, 34–35, 51–52, 67, 68, 72–73
Louisiana Purchase, 3
Louisville, Ky., 14, 50, 52, 60, 74, 81, 110
Louisville and Portland Canal, 39, 110

Mackenzie River, 163
Mail service, 74
Mexican War, 102
Mississippi River, 2, 3, 4, 32, 70, 91; course of, 100; model, 109; passenger service on, 76, 80; snags in, 81, 87; steamboats on, 1, 5, 12, 14, 41, 46, 61, 69, 74, 81
Missouri River, 3, 4, 74–76
Monongahela River (the Mon), 2, 3, 7, 8, 9, 10, 13, 45
Mud Island, 109
Museum of History and Technology, 110

Napoleon (steamboat), 73, 74
Natchez, Miss., 5, 19, 36, 74, 90
Natchitoches (settlement), 91–92
National Road, 45
New Orleans (steamboat), 14, 15, 34, 41, 47
New Orleans, La., 61, 63, 68, 74, 81; port city, 4, 5, 6; in War of 1812, 8–9, 11, 13, 16–31

Ohio (steamboat), 62, 73, 74
Ohio River, 2, 4, 13, 14, 41, 45, 50, 67, 70, 72, 73, 74, 81; passenger service on, 76; snags in, 84, 85, 86–87
Ohio River Museum, 109
Oliver Evans (ship), 63

Pacific Railroad Company, 102
Paddlewheels, 10, 44, 51, 76, 79
Pearl (steamboat), 91
Perry, Oliver Hazard, 54
Pittsburgh, Pa., 2, 4, 13, 74
Point Harmar, 56
Polk, James, 102
Portland, 52, 60
Post Boy (mail boat), 74

Railroad, 4, 76, 102
Red River, 30, 87–89, 90–98, 99
Reel, Harriet, 100, 101
Reel, John, 100
Rivers (U.S.): free navigation, 31, 51–52, 54, 63, 66, 67–70, 71–72; transportation on, 1, 4, 31, 54, 82, 98, 103

St. Louis, Mo., 3, 74, 100, 101, 102
Shippingport, Ky., 14, 38, 62, 67, 69
Shreve, Florence, 102, 103
Shreve, Hampden Zane, 41, 53
Shreve, Harriet, 41, 100
Shreve, Henry Miller, 1, 2; boat-building companies, 3–4, 43–47, 48–49; boats designed, built by, 1, 43–44, 45–47, 49–57, 60, 70, 73–74, 76–80, 83, 84–87, 109; business ventures, 100–01, 102; chronology, 104–07; early life, 2; illness, death of, 102–03; inventions, 2, 49–50, 74, 83, 85–86, legacy of, 103; marriage, family, 4, 31, 41, 50, 53, 100, 101–03
Shreve, Col. Israel, 2, 3
Shreve, Lydia Rodgers, 102
Shreve, Mary (d. of H.S), 102
Shreve, Mary (1st wife of H.S.), 7, 41, 44, 48, 50, 60–61, 100, 102
Shreve, Rebecca, 41, 100
Shreveport, 95, 97, 98
Snag boats, 2, 85–89, 90–98, 99
Snags (sawyers), 10, 11, 14, 31, 81–87
Souvenir (steamboat), 91

Steam engines, 44, 49, 50, 110; high-pressure, 38, 42–43, 46–47, 50, 54–55, 61, 63, 67, 73, 76; safety valves, 43, 46–47, 59, 60, 61
Steamboats, 1, 4–5, 8, 12, 40, 41, 46, 61–62, 63, 69, 70, 73–76, 96, 100–01, 103, 110; lost to snags, 81–82
Supreme Court, 70, 82

Texas, 87, 97
Texas Revolution, 97
Tyler, John, 99

United States, 3, 4; western, 74–76, 87
U.S. Army Corps of Engineers, 82, 84, 98
U.S. Congress, 82, 84, 86, 95–96, 97, 98
U.S. Superintendent of Western River Improvements, 84, 99, 100

Vesuvius (steamboat), 11, 12, 15, 16, 18, 30, 34, 37, 61

War of 1812, 5, 8–9, 16–31, 54, 74
Washington, George, 2, 52
Washington (steamboat), 52–57, 58–70, 73–76, 101, 103
Wheeling Creek, 45, 50
White, George, 45–46, 47, 48, 50–52, 55
W. P. Snyder (towboat), 109

Youghiogheny River (the Yough), 2